THE SIPSTER'S POCKET GUIDE
TO 50 MORE MUST-TRY ONTARIO WINES

VOLUME 2

VOL.
2

THE
Sipster's

POCKET GUIDE
TO 50 MORE MUST-TRY
ONTARIO WINES

LUKE WHITTALL

TOUCHWOOD

The information in this book is true and complete to the best of the
author's knowledge. All recommendations are made without guarantee
on the part of the author or the publisher.

Copy edited by Senica Maltese
Cover and interior design by Sydney Barnes

Photography by Luke Whittall, with the following exceptions: pages 19,
21, 23, 27, 33, 35, 37, 45, 57, 61, 65, 79, 81, 83, 85,
89, 95, 117, 123 (provided by the wineries)

CATALOGUING DATA AVAILABLE FROM LIBRARY AND ARCHIVES CANADA
ISBN 9781771514439 (softcover)
ISBN 9781771514446 (electronic)

TouchWood Editions acknowledges that the land on which we live and
work is within the traditional territories of the Lkwungen (Esquimalt
and Songhees), Malahat, Pacheedaht, Scia'new, T'Sou-ke, and ẉsÁNEĆ
(Pauquachin, Tsartlip, Tsawout, and Tseycum) peoples.

We acknowledge the financial support of the Government of Canada
through the Canada Book Fund and of the Province of British Columbia
through the Book Publishing Tax Credit.

This book was produced using FSC®-certified,
acid-free papers, processed chlorine free, and printed
with soya-based inks.

Printed in China

28 27 26 25 24 1 2 3 4 5

To Ann Sperling, who makes amazing wines and was the first person I interviewed for my first book nearly a decade ago. Thank you for being so gracious with your time.

sipster

sip·ster | \ sip-stər \

: one who observes, seeks, and sets taste trends of sipping beverages, such as wine, spirits, tea, and coffee, outside of the mainstream.

CONTENTS

INTRODUCTION

Welcome back to the wonderful world of the sipster! If you don't consider yourself a sipster, this book will illuminate what is possible for you through wine appreciation. Plus, it's just fun!

If you haven't read Volume 1, there is no need to run out and buy a copy (although I hope you do at some point). Volume 2 doesn't replace or update Volume 1; the Sipster's Pocket Guides remain timeless, casual wine reading no matter when you pick them up. In these pages, you will learn about some of the most amazing Ontario wines ever produced by some of the most amazing people ever to produce wine in the region. Hopefully, this will inspire you to seek out some of them on your next trip to wine country or the local liquor store. Even if you don't find the exact wines I've written about here, you may enjoy another wine in a featured winery's portfolio. Drinking wine is proxy for adventure; you can "travel" all over the world just by sipping this amazing liquid. If you live in Ontario, you are lucky to have at least one world-class wine region, if not more, close at hand for you to explore. Bring your Sipster's Pocket Guide along and let it help you navigate this exciting adventure.

Where will your next glass take you?

WHY I AM NOT A WINE CRITIC

People sometimes refer to me as a wine critic, and each time, I become a little more offended. That is *really* not what I do. Yes, I write about wine, but that is very different.

I write about wine like a music writer writes about music, or a baseball writer writes about baseball. Each of these writers documents something they love. You might say that writing about wine is a passion of mine, but I don't think that adequately explains it. I love to cook food on my barbecue, but I don't want to write about that. Someone else might, and that's great. I also love riding a motorcycle but, again, it doesn't inspire the words to flow. For me, it's wine. Wine is my *why*, as Simon Sinek would say.

This amazing liquid can foster amazing experiences with friends; simply smelling and tasting it can evoke images and sentiments. I can't make wine and share it with you (I'm not qualified for that, although I have worked as a winery cellar hand) so instead, I write about it and share that. If what I write inspires you to seek out some of these wines or visit one of the wineries, that's fantastic, but that's not really why I write. I'm not here to try to sell you any particular wines.

Maya Angelou's famous quote, "At the end of the day people won't remember what you said or did, they will remember how you made them feel," is equally applicable to wine. I believe that people remember a wine not because it has hints of strawberries streaked with oregano on the nose; they remember it because of how it made them feel. People remember wines because of the experience they had when they drank it. Where were they? Who were they with? What were they talking about? These factors are far more important than knowing that a wine had 18 months in French oak barrels with 50% of them being new from the oak forests of Limousin, where the trees were harvested by angels during a full moon. When you are sipping a wine with your lover in the tub, will the experience be ruined by a wine that lacks depth on the midpalate? No, it won't (although it might ruin the experience if you decide to bring that kind of information up during a relaxing soak).

Traditional wine writing is so hung up on the technical aspects of wine that the experiential elements get completely ignored. This starts early for people who, as wine students, are taught to break down every wine into its theoretical component parts and ascribe a value judgment to it without knowing anything specific (such as each wine's provenance or price) beforehand. Yet for most people, wine is experiential, making them feel something regardless of the technical details. A beautiful wine experience cannot be directly attributed to the smooth texture created by malolactic fermentation in neutral oak barrels. Some learned wine professionals and astute wine students understand this. Even though they are trained to look for these technical things and can recognize them when they taste them, they aren't necessarily going to enjoy the wine more because of it. Technical stuff means nothing to most people, so why are wine blogs, books, and articles filled with so much technical data?

Below, I have created two examples to demonstrate how traditional wine writing would look when applied to another subject. Here is a concert review, written in the style of a wine reviewer:

54.40 LIVE AT THE BASE 31 DRILL HALL, PICTON, ONTARIO—AUGUST 5, 2023

Lead singer Neil Osborne wowed the crowd from the first steady beats of "Easy to Love" through to the final chords of "Love You All." The rhythm section of bassist Brad Merritt (using an early '70s Precision Bass through an Ampeg SVT) and drummer Matt Johnson (on a well-worn Yamaha kit and Sabian cymbals) provided the solid structure on which the entire band was able to perform the full 90-minute set. Guitarist Dave Genn favoured a mid-'80s Stratocaster for most of the set, which was a surprise given the tonal characteristics of the swamp ash body and maple neck of the guitar. He made it work well with a small array of analogue stomp boxes positioned within easy reach below his microphone. The stage was placed correctly within the confines of the room but some acoustic dead spots did prevent an optimal listener experience for some patrons, particularly in the back corners, which had partially obstructed sightlines. The energy from the band was still impressive, considering they have been doing this since the 1980s. There is strong potential for their collaboration to continue for a few more years yet. All in all, a solid concert. 93 points.

Or if a wine reviewer wrote about a hockey game:

BOSTON VS. TORONTO AT THE AIR CANADA CENTRE

The ice wasn't the only thing frozen at the ACC last night. Although the ambient air temperature hovered around 14 degrees, it was pretty clear that Boston goaltender Jeremy Swayman had every intention of freezing Toronto out. Swayman's stick was made from aspen, sourced from the Crested Butte region in Colorado, with birch lamination for reinforcement, making it lightweight but durable enough to maintain consistent control throughout the game. The "Little Ball of Hate" Brad Marchand scored the winning goal on a slapper using his Sherwood stick made with oak sourced from the forests of Missouri, which allowed him just the right amount of flex to get it past Toronto goalie Joseph Woll. Though Toronto didn't win, the team still showed up strong, winning the majority of the faceoffs and controlling the puck with great complexity. The balance was still off since the offence struggled to keep pace with Boston's top lines. Though the game ended 2–1 for Boston, the excitement of it made watching this game a reasonable experience. Watch live only—not worth PVR space. 86 points.

Sound ridiculous? It really is. Traditional wine writing is so bogged down with the technical aspects of the wine's origins that the whole point of it seems lost. After listening to their technical assessments, wine importer Terry Theise used to ask wine critics the toughest question of all: Did you like the wine? More often than not, the critic was unable to answer convincingly, likely because they weren't expecting the question; they weren't trained to answer it when they were learning to evaluate wine. They were trained to look at wine objectively with criteria that they could objectively measure (theoretically, at least). The Sipster's Guides are not about objectivity ("This wine is fantastic because . . ."), and they are not about subjectivity either ("I love this wine because . . ."). They are my attempt to transcribe an experience from one artistic medium (wine) to another (writing).

I have a few hopes for those who read any of my Sipster's Pocket Guides. First, I hope that you have as much fun reading about the wines as I did tasting and writing about them. I hope you can sense my joy throughout the book.

Second, I hope that you seek out some of the wines or wineries featured here. There is a reason that I've chosen to write about *these* wines. They are made by wineries that produce intriguing vintages that will enliven your life with a beautiful imbibing experience. Some of them have great stories of their own to tell. You may even find yourself planning your next trip around a visit to some of these beautiful places. Touring Ontario wineries is not as far removed as you might think, even if you feel like Niagara is a little too far to travel. There are other wineries scattered around the province—from Glengarry County in the far east, Pelee Island in the southwest, and even Georgian Bay in the north—all of which are absolutely worth experiencing for yourself. Please visit them and take your Sipster's Pocket Guide along for the adventure.

Third, I hope that you share your own wine experiences with other people, helping to create a culture around wine that can be passed on to friends, family, and even future generations. Perhaps years from now, a son or daughter will learn that their parents met at an event at 13th Street Winery. They may even be used to seeing their wines on the dinner table. But, they won't know, or even care, that one of those wines scored 90 points.

At the back of this book, I have included a few pages of official Sipster's Wine Notes that you can use to help you keep track of your favourite wines as you experience them.

LIVING THE SENSORY LIFE— SIPSTER TRAINING

I believe that we, as individuals, have different levels of sensitivity when it comes to sensory experiences. We all experience things differently, and I think that this is the root of a fundamental flaw in the way that we traditionally communicate about wine. Bland tasting notes and random point scores assume that we all have the same sensitivity, tasting experience, and intentions when we sit down to enjoy a glass of wine. It reminds me of that "deep" question that seems to circulate in high schools: *Is the colour blue that I see the same colour blue that you see?* If one person is slightly colour-blind, clearly the answer is no.

Instead of visual colour, think about any of the other things that we can sense as humans: pitch, texture, flavour, scent. Do we all have the same sensitivities to these things? Do we all have the same ability to use the information that we get from these senses? Do we all care about them in the same measure? Some people are more ticklish than others. Elite athletes are able to respond to physical sensations on a much higher level and can use that information differently than those who are not as well trained.

If beauty is in the eye of the beholder, then surely beauty must be sensed in different measures by different people. These differences in sensitivity are what make us all unique individuals. How then can we expect everyone to learn about something as complex as wine in the same way? I believe this assumption of sameness is one of the biggest problems in New World (a.k.a. non-European) wine industries. Not only are consumers coming from a diversity of backgrounds and cultures, but the producers are also similarly all over the map (literally and metaphorically). Producers in Ontario are trying to balance what they like in wine, what they want to produce, and what they are able to produce. Consumers are trying to understand the myriad of grapes, flavours, and textures that wineries offer. No wonder everyone is confused.

Learning what we like is relatively simple but, shockingly, it's not something we're taught as kids. We are taught that we have to eat vegetables we don't like. We are taught that our preferences don't matter. We have to eat so we have energy and grow up healthy. Parenting styles may vary, but typically, parents create the food for the family to enjoy. It's the parents' tastes (based on culture, finances, and personal preference) that dictate what their kids will eat. Kids' preferences be damned. It is only later, as teenagers, that we realize that we can act on our own preferences, but the sudden rush of making choices can be overwhelming.

Wine is unique among food items in that there is so much choice available to us. The variation in styles and flavours is huge. Imagine a grocery store stocking 80–100 different boxes of crackers from various producers and in various styles. The average cracker section of a grocery store may have 10, maybe 15, varieties. Even a small liquor store will probably have more than a dozen different bottles of wine. The choice is daunting. How can a novice sipster possibly learn all of those styles?

This is where we can all benefit from a little training. Sipster training is a kind of boot camp for your taste buds. A pep talk for your palate. A strength test for your sniffer. We can train our senses of smell and taste daily with the things we eat and drink. However, instead of eating the same things every day and not paying much attention to them, why not take the time to sense as much as you can?

Take everyday food items out of their context to evaluate them in a focused way, comparing multiple versions side by side. Focus on what makes each variation unique. One type of trail mix may be more fruity. Another more sweet, or salty, or savoury. One might have a firmer, crispier texture. Paying attention to the elements that make each version stand out from the others can be an amazing experience that helps whip your palate into shape. Try this exercise with some of the following foods, and remember: the key to knowing how to taste wine like a sipster is not to study wine but to study yourself. Learn what you like, not what everyone else likes!

POTATO CHIPS

This is an easy and fun one to do with friends, but you can do it on your own as well.

Buy three or more bags of potato chips of the same flavour—regular, salt and vinegar, barbecue, whatever—but from different brands such as Lay's, Ruffles, Old Dutch, or whatever is available. Tortilla chips also work well for this. Place them in bowls so that nobody can tell which brands belong to each bowl.

Now taste them individually and take time to note the differences that you sense between them. Writing your thoughts somewhere is a good idea, especially if you have a lot of different chips to taste. Pay attention to the qualities that you get from each one. What is the texture like, and do you have a preference for one of them? How salty are they? Are some crispier than others? Are the flavours equally strong in all of them? Does one stand out to you more than the others? Focus on all the sensations that each chip presents to you, from appearance to thickness to texture to flavour. Anything that you can sense is fair game.

When everyone in the group is done, compare your notes. Did any chips stand out and, if so, what set them apart? If you tasted with a group, was there a consensus about which chips were most preferred? Were there any common descriptors?

HONEY

This is a slightly more difficult experiment to execute, but it's a fantastic experience if you can manage it. You may need to visit a good honey producer, but even purchasing three different types of honey from the store can set you up for an interesting experience.

You may think all honeys taste the same. It's just sugar, right? Wrong. Honey has an amazing array of flavour variations based on the pollen the bees used to make it. Honey made from a hive located in an apple orchard will taste very different from honey from a hive located near a berry patch, or a lavender farm, or the site of a recent forest fire! The variations in flavour and sweetness are truly amazing. This is a true test of your palate since the variations will be found less in presentation and texture and more in flavours and nuances.

Line up as many honeys as you can find in small bowls. Dip a toothpick or small fork into each honey and taste it. Just like with the chips, spend as much time as you can with each one, being aware of each honey's flavour, texture, sweetness, and overall desirability. Which one was your favourite and why? Did one have a flavour that you didn't like as much? Were the differences between them very subtle or extreme?

HOT SAUCES

Live out your *Hot Ones* dream and try a series of hot sauces in sequence. What they do on that show is basically the same thing as a traditional wine tasting but with a lot more panic and occasional sobbing. Although a sip of wine will never physically hurt you (barring any allergies) like some hot sauces might, tasting a range of hot sauces in one sitting can be a great tasting experience.

Line up three or more food items. The more foods you have, the more different sauces you can experience. Chicken wings are the tried and true favourite, of course, but hard-boiled eggs, grilled cheese sandwich slices, roasted cauliflower, or plain tortilla chips will also work. The best experience will use something small and bite sized. The more sauces you have to try, the smaller the portion of each should be.

If you happen to know how hot each sauce is (Scoville Heat Units—or SHU—is the scale that measures a food's spiciness), line them up from the lowest SHU score to the highest. This is very similar to wine tasting, where tasters generally prefer to taste from the lightest, driest, or least acidic wines to the fullest, sweetest, or most acidic ones. Going in this direction makes it more likely that you will experience each hot sauce for what it is and not have a less intense sauce overpowered by a spicier one that's come before. If you aren't sure, let your nose guide you. Spicier hot sauces will probably have a more immediate intensity when you smell them.

Try to evaluate what you are experiencing with each hot sauce. Do it in a way that you will remember. If you need to write things down, write them down. Talk about the experience with others as you go. It probably won't be hard to determine and agree on which one is the spiciest, but which one has the most appealing flavours? Did one have a texture that you liked better? Was there a vinegary quality to any of them? Did a hot sauce enhance or detract from the flavour of the food, or the experience of eating the food? Pick out your favourite and discuss it with your friends. Did everyone agree?

These food items are only suggestions. You could try lots of other things like crackers or ice cream or pizza. All you really need to do is pay a little more attention to what you are eating. Out of context tastings like this are a good way to learn about your preferences and provide a wonderful opportunity to try new things. The world is there to be experienced. Practising sensory awareness can help you experience things more fully. That's living like a true sipster! Once you've got exercises like this down, the next step is to pay more attention to everything you sense over the course of your day. You may be shocked by what you notice. The world is a sensory powerhouse. Enjoy it!

A NOTE ON HOW THE WINES WERE TASTED

Just like in previous volumes of this guide, these wines were enjoyed in their natural environment: with meals, on special occasions, with food and friends, and using various styles of wineglasses. I used just about any kind of glass that was designed for drinking *wine*. No mugs, tumblers, or juice cups were used. I am not trying to prove a point about any particular stemware philosophy but rather enjoy wine idiomatically. It's not always worth getting out the big Riedel Double Magnums to enjoy that big red with dinner, but sometimes it's really fun to do just that.

I followed some protocols to give each wine the chance to taste its best. Wines were served at their proper serving temperatures. White wines were chilled and reds were not. Canned wines were poured into wineglasses. All wines were paired with a suitable food and occasion, and my impressions of the wines were written down immediately, usually with some still in my glass.

HOW THE WINES ARE PRESENTED

WINERY AND WINE NAME

WINERY PRICE: ♀ = < $10
♀ ♀ = $10–$20
♀ ♀ ♀ = $20–$30
♀ ♀ ♀ ♀ = $30–$40
♀ ♀ ♀ ♀ ♀ = $40–$50
BODY: LIGHT/MEDIUM/FULL
SWEETNESS: DRY/OFF-DRY/MEDIUM/SWEET/LUSCIOUS
ATTITUDE: THE WINE'S PERSONALITY

Pair with: Foods, moods, and occasions

WINERY PRICE: This is the approximate price range of the wine, pre-tax, as listed on the winery's website. Prices are subject to change at the whim of the winery, of course, so none of the prices listed here are set in stone. They will give you a general sense of what you can expect to pay.

BODY: When wine people talk about the body of a wine, they are referring to the perceived fullness or texture of the wine. I like to describe it in terms of milk. Skim milk feels light and watery. Move up to 2% milk and the texture feels a bit fuller. Homogenized milk will be even fuller, and 10% cream even more so. Wine is the same way—watery and thin or thick and full. It has nothing to do with the intensity of the flavour, only the sensation of the texture.

Why does this matter? It matters because it affects what you pair the wine with—foods or occasions. The weight of the wine needs to match the weight of the food and the occasion. Looking for a great wine to have for your après-ski beef bourguignon? A cold bottle of Sauvignon Blanc won't fit the situation, no matter how great a wine it is. A rich Syrah or Merlot, on the other hand, will warm you up and taste great with the food too. Save the Sauvignon Blanc for the salad course at your next formal dinner.

SWEETNESS: During my years in wine sales, I found this was usually one of the first three questions that customers asked (along with "What are the grape varieties?" and "How much is it?"). It is also one of the most misunderstood factors, as most people associate dry alcoholic beverages with a thinner texture. Let me try to clear this up. Dry means "no sugar" (i.e., not sweet). Off-dry means that there is a little bit of sugar, usually to balance the high acidity of a wine. Some people may taste a bit of sweetness while others won't but will notice a more rounded texture.

Winemakers need to be aware of a wine's sweetness because sugar and acidity have to be balanced. Think of it like lemon juice. If you squeeze a lemon to make lemonade, what do you need to make it drinkable? Sugar! Sugar is what balances the high acidity of the lemon juice, and voila—a refreshing beverage on a hot summer day. If there isn't enough sugar, it will taste sour. Too much sugar, and it tastes cloying. Getting that balance right is the key.

Ontario wines naturally have more acid compared with those made in hotter wine-growing regions, so a little residual sugar can make them balanced. Right now, it is more acceptable for white wines to have higher levels of residual sugar than reds. As such, Ontario-made red wines are generally fermented completely dry, with no residual sugar at all.

If the vintage is successful and the winemaker has done a good job, most people won't even notice that there is sugar in a wine. It will simply taste well made. Sugar is not bad or good. It is there for balance. We've had a couple of generations of wine lovers who grew up thinking that they were not supposed to like sweet wines. If you are concerned about getting headaches from sweeter wines, consider drinking less in an evening. Problem solved.

ATTITUDE: This is where my wine descriptions really start to diverge from the norm. The characteristics mentioned so far are based on more measurable factors, with body being the description of texture and sweetness being an assessment of sugar that can be accurately measured through laboratory analysis. Aroma descriptors are less easily measurable, and writers must rely on similes to get the point across. One could say that a wine smells like blackcurrants, dried mangoes, or tennis balls, but that doesn't mean that the wine actually has those aromas deliberately built into it (though if you are new to wine, I can see how easy that is to assume). It is also one person's perception of that wine, someone who we assume is adequately qualified to make those assessments. Were they trained as a winemaker, a sommelier, or an educator? With the Court of Master Sommeliers? International Sommelier Guild? Wine & Spirit Education Trust? To what level? Does that even matter?

Training inconsistencies aside, using only aromatic descriptors to describe a wine is limiting when wines can be described using other linguistic devices. Attitudes, images, and metaphors are way more fun and can help us understand the wine more thoroughly. Lots of wines have "aromas of strawberries and dried herbs," but only this one can be described as being "like relaxing in a natural hot springs in the mountains." Some wines are hidden or coy, while others are bombastic or vivacious. Wines are not just wines; they can be like people. They can have attitudes and personalities. The ultimate wine pairing is when the right wine is matched to the right situation.

PAIR WITH: Wines are almost always paired with foods, although even this is a relatively recent phenomenon in the history of wine consumption. Suggestions for food pairings are common in the marketing material provided by wineries, as well as in the banter spouted by eager wine-shop sales staff. There are many books and college courses dedicated to food and wine pairing. Learning the techniques is a great way to increase your enjoyment of wine at meals.

But what if you don't happen to have duck confit and cherry gastrique prepared for dinner tonight and just want to enjoy a wine on its own? What if you want to have a glass while watching the sunset? What about the best wine for a relaxing bath or impromptu picnic?

Matching wine to food is important, but matching it to the occasion should enhance and deepen the enjoyment of both more effectively. At its most basic, a truly great pairing is when the wine and its accompaniment mutually reinforce each other without one overshadowing the other. The wine should make the food taste better, and the food should make the wine taste better. The same goes for the occasion: the wine should help make it that much more memorable.

In this book, I list possibilities for foods, moods, and occasions that I believe will pair beautifully with these wines. You can also search through the "pairings" entry in the index at the back of the book to find the perfect wine.

If you are drawn to some of these wines, I encourage you to seek them out for yourself. Make your own notes about them. This is one of the many things that make wine fun. Happy sipping!

SPARKLING WINES

As with most wine styles from Ontario, I've noticed that the sparkling category is a tad underappreciated. It's almost too easy to default to international wines when putting together a shopping list for your next trip to the LCBO. The wine world makes this the easiest option because they have successfully made nearly generic names out of successful regions. The classic example is Champagne; people often identify a sparkling wine as "champagne" when they aren't really talking about the specific style made in Champagne. Cava and Prosecco have almost attempted the same thing but without using a regional name, and they are succeeding. Enterprising wineries on Vancouver Island have developed a cute name for the sparkling wines produced there—Charme de l'Île—and any wineries on Vancouver Island or the Gulf Islands can produce wines under that name. It's only been a few years so the jury is still out on if it will catch on.

Until the day arrives when you can ask your partner to pick up a bottle of Beamsville or maybe Crémant d'Escarpment[1] on the way home, Ontario sparkling wines may always be an afterthought. The wineries shouldn't be blamed for this. Deciding to make sparkling wine comes with a sizable investment in specialized equipment.

That's why it is even more important to support the wineries that do. They clearly really want to do it. That kind of enthusiasm normally makes for some exciting wines, which is exactly what I've experienced with all of the Ontario sparkling wines I've tried recently.

Next time, instead of Champagne, consider popping the top on a bottle of Niagara.

1 How about Crem-Dee for short?

As the evening progresses, it will tell jokes that make everyone laugh.

DIVERGENCE

RIESLING BRUT
VQA LINCOLN LAKESHORE VQA

DIVERGENCE RIESLING BRUT

WINERY PRICE: ♙ ♙ ♙
BODY: LIGHT
SWEETNESS: DRY
ATTITUDE: CUT TO THE CHASE

Pair with: Anything (literally anything), holiday gatherings

Some wines are secretive while others remain aloof or austere, hiding themselves until the perfect moment strikes. It can take minutes swirling in the glass, hours in a decanter, or years in the cellar before these wines are ready to make themselves known.

Good thing this *isn't* one of those wines.

This beautiful sparkling wine will arrive to the party slightly later than everyone else. If they don't know many people, they'll approach each person to introduce themselves, shaking their hand while looking them directly in the eyes with a confidence that is inspiring. This wine will lead by example, smiling each time you sip. As the evening progresses, it will tell jokes that make everyone laugh. This wine is an absolute charmer.

For the tentative wine drinker, this is confidence-inspiring. You can do no wrong when it comes to mixing and matching with foods or occasions. Go ahead and be you!

If you can't find something fun to do at a fair, you may have a fun allergy of some kind.

FANCY FARM GIRL FROSTY FIZZ

WINERY PRICE: 🍷 🍷
BODY: LIGHT
SWEETNESS: OFF-DRY
ATTITUDE: FUN

Pair with: Flatbread pizza, focaccia, frolicking at a fair with friends

With a name and branding like this wine, it's hard to argue that it's anything but fun. There are a lot of F-words that I could use to describe this wine, but *fun* is still the most applicable. This wine is more than appropriately labelled, which means that it's easy to recognize on the shelf. Anybody who enjoys a fluttery frizzy will find something to love about it.

Pairings aside, the fact remains that this wine wouldn't have the same appeal were it less masterfully made. It's an experience that anyone can enjoy, like a county fair (another F-word!). If you can't find something fun to do at a fair, you may have a fun allergy of some kind. There are animals, farm machinery, competitions, midway rides, food and bevvies, and cheap prizes that will probably fall apart before you reach the car.

Fairs are a celebration of farms and the farming lifestyle. I am often reminded of this lifestyle when I sip a new wine for the first time. Wine, perhaps more than any other food, is linked to its birthplace and to the people who grew its grapes. Even if this wine didn't have a fancy name, it would still spark an authentic experience.

It will never leave you in the lurch or refuse to compromise.

FRED WINES PRIMROSÉ

WINERY PRICE: ♟ ♟ ♟ ♟
BODY: LIGHT
SWEETNESS: DRY
ATTITUDE: TRUSTING

Pair with: Light cheeses, scallops, besties

When it comes to relationships, trust is slow to gain and quick to lose. Everyone perceives trust a little differently, which can make for disagreements and even conflicts. When you find someone you connect with so deeply that the trust is implicit and the respect is mutual, you've found someone special indeed.

This is a wine you can trust without fail. It will deliver on its promises and always tell you the truth. It will never leave you in the lurch or refuse to compromise. It's as upstanding as they come, a wine that will be there for you no matter what.

"How can a wine do that?" you may ask, eyebrows furrowed.

Trust comes from many different places, but no matter what, it must be mutual. You need to trust this wine first and then, only then, it will trust you back, giving you such beautiful aromas and flavours that you will want to cuddle up with your glass and tell it about all of the things that have been bothering you lately.

Trust. Sip. Enjoy.

But damn if it
doesn't just fit right
in with the flavour of
birthday cake and the
occasional sound of
crocodile tears.

PELLER ESTATES ICE CUVÉE ROSÉ

WINERY PRICE: 🍷 🍷 🍷 🍷
BODY: MEDIUM
SWEETNESS: MEDIUM SWEET
ATTITUDE: ROLLER COASTER

Pair with: Spicy pad Thai, salty cheeses, kids' birthday parties

If you have the pleasure of throwing a kid's birthday party, this is the perfect wine to offer the other parents. Yes, it is pink. It's also a little sweet. But damn if it doesn't just fit right in with the flavour of birthday cake and the occasional sound of crocodile tears.

Why does pairing wine with the occasion matter? Because sipsters are always conscious of context. An austere or hidden wine (an "Oh, this wine will be great in five years" kind of wine) is suitable for an occasion where people have the time to really dig in and explore it, such as in a wine shop or tasting seminar. A simple wine with less complexity that's ready to enjoy the minute it's bottled wouldn't be interesting in those circumstances, but it would be fantastic at an informal reception or casual party.

This wine doesn't fall into either of these categories. There is no austerity here, but it isn't so simple that it should be written off as a casual party wine. Not every wine can do it all like this one can. Essentially, it's a fun wine without being the cheap, one-dimensional slosh that high school kids in Quebec used to buy for their friends who don't like beer.[2] This is the real stuff with all of the complexity and nuance that sipsters expect from a quality wine, but with the added bonus of being accessibly tasty.

---

2 Allegedly. I heard a rumour about it. Once. Like, a while ago, maybe . . .

Maybe you've just renovated a room but haven't moved any of the furnishings in yet.

PENINSULA RIDGE
TINY BUBBLES SPARKLING WINE

WINERY PRICE: 🍷 🍷
BODY: MEDIUM
SWEETNESS: OFF-DRY
ATTITUDE: CLEANSING

Pair with: Chicken wings, popcorn, setting up new spaces

Successfully preparing to do something new invites a particular kind of energy, ripe with potential. When you've just set up your new home office and are looking at the clean desk—free of sticky notes, pens, coffee rings, and other clutter—the work you plan to undertake there feels fresh. Maybe you've just renovated a room but haven't moved any of the furnishings in yet. It might even be something as simple as cleaning your vehicle for a trip you've been anticipating. There is a lot of potential in these moments, and what could be more exciting?

This beautiful sparkling wine embodies the energy of potential. The first sip is refreshing, clearing away any of the tastes lingering in your mouth (sipsters and chefs call this "palate cleansing," and it's a big part of all good wine and food pairings).

The second sip brings the first whisper of change. You may even question your first impression of the wine. *Did it really taste this smooth before? Now it is even smoother. Wow!* With the third sip, the beautiful fruit flavours will begin to reveal themselves, slowly. The more you sip and snack, the more enjoyable the experience, and the more potential energy you will release for your taste buds.

You're ready for whatever comes next. Enjoy the journey!

Everything feels effortless and takes very little conscious thought.

TAWSE SPARK SPARKLING WINE

WINERY PRICE: ♈ ♈ ♈
BODY: MEDIUM
SWEETNESS: OFF-DRY
ATTITUDE: THE ZONE

Pair with: Nachos, BBQ potato chips, first dates

This wine is in the zone. It's perfectly dialled in and ready for anything, and you need to be prepared for that when you pop the cork.

If being in "the zone" isn't something you've felt recently, let's reintroduce this fantastic experience. Remember that heightened sense of focus, so intense it's almost like you don't have to think about what you're doing anymore. Your skills are working on autopilot, and you're along for the ride. Athletes and musicians often talk about this state of being. When they get in the zone, everything feels effortless and takes very little conscious thought. Everything flows naturally.

Wine can take you into the zone as well, especially if a great food pairing is part of the experience. Sparkling wines generally trend toward versatility, but in this case, you have *lots* of room to be adventurous. Having smoked prime rib tonight? How about homemade pizza with spicy sausage? Risotto, perhaps? Of course, you can indulge in seafood and all of the classic sparkling wine pairings, too. All of these are possibilities that will bring you into the zone of a great pairing experience. It's also perfect for that first date, which will get you out of the "friend zone"!

WHITE WINES

Ontario is uniquely positioned in the world of wine as a place that can grow almost any kind of white wine grape it wants. And yet, the most focus seems to fall on four main white grape varieties. Chardonnay and Riesling are far and away the dominant grapes grown for white wine here. Pinot Gris and Sauvignon Blanc follow close behind with many under-the-radar favourites. Sipsters know that Ontario whites are a diverse lot, which is a huge part of the appeal. Every bottle is an adventure waiting to happen. Finding a pairing that works for you is the most important thing.

Like sparkling wines, white wines have a reputation for being consumed on their own without food pairings. Unlike sparkling wines, which are associated with celebrating something, white wines are viewed as more workaday and often aren't tied to a particular function. If anything, they are relegated to the bottom of the pile for formalities. Sparkling wines get held up on New Year's Eves while white wines get held up on nights when *The Bachelor* is on. Red wines always get paired with the main course while white wines get the hors d'oeuvres or maybe the salad course, making them forgotten by the end of the meal.

Sipsters know that white wines can be every bit as challenging as red wines. They know that they can also be as seriously complex, interesting, and worthy of attention as any other type of wine and on any other occasion.

This is where Ontario white wines can really stand out.

You have to get
up and tend to the
turntable at regular
intervals.

13TH STREET WINERY PINOT GRIS

WINERY PRICE: 🍷 🍷 🍷
BODY: LIGHT
SWEETNESS: DRY
ATTITUDE: ATTENTIVE

Pair with: Manchego, grilled white fish, weekend afternoons in the summer

WHITE

There's a big difference between listening to music on a playlist and listening to music on a turntable with a vinyl record spinning on a platter. Leaving aside questions of sound quality (which are not obvious to everyone), different media require different levels of our active attention.

Playing music from a streaming playlist takes very little attention. You make a single decision when you hit play and then you can just go about your business until the playlist stops or your device runs out of juice. The music will just keep playing regardless of how much attention you pay it. For social gatherings or background music at work, this is ideal. The music itself isn't supposed to be your main focus.

Playing music on vinyl is a little more involved. You have to get up and tend to the turntable at regular intervals—every five songs on vintage vinyl or every three on modern records with longer songs. You have to remain attentive just to keep the music going. When the music stops, whatever you are doing is put temporarily on hold as you go to the turntable and make another choice—flip the disc, choose another, or stop the music altogether.

This wine requires your attention, but you'll be rewarded with every sniff and sip. The aromas are particularly fetching and, like having to tend to that turntable every 20 minutes, you'll find yourself with your nose in the glass regularly. Turn the record and pour yourself some more.

You feel invincible, destined to take whatever silliness this so-called real world throws at you.

16 MILE CELLAR
TENACITY CHARDONNAY

WINERY PRICE: 🍷 🍷 🍷 🍷
BODY: MEDIUM
SWEETNESS: DRY
ATTITUDE: PREPARED

Pair with: Poutine, lobster rolls, reunions

This wine has the exhilaration of a fresh accomplishment. In the moments after graduating from high school, college, or university when you're told that you're ready for "the real world," you may swell with a sudden surge of energy that makes you feel invincible, destined to take whatever silliness this so-called real world throws at you.

"Why is that feeling a good thing in a wine?" you may ask. That's fine. Ask that. It's a great question.

Eventually, the post-graduation exhilaration wears off (sorry—spoiler alert for Gen Z). And while it doesn't disappear completely, it does dissipate until the energy is no longer potent enough to drive your decisions. After a few years, you may have even forgotten that you were all that excited about "the real world" to begin with. By the time you learn what "the real world" is, you may have forgotten what you thought it was.

Sometimes it's good to be reminded of how far you've come and how much you've accomplished. This wine may even remind you of "the real world" you once imagined, revealing that you're a lot closer to your dreams than you realized.

As soon as that wavy red line appears, I have the unhinged desire to correct the error rather than admit defeat to the computer.

BELLA TERRA VINEYARDS FUMÉ BLANC

WINERY PRICE: 🍷 🍷 🍷 🍷
BODY: MEDIUM
SWEETNESS: DRY
ATTITUDE: DRIVEN

Pair with: Spinach salad with goat cheese, pasta with herbs, writing poetry in your mind

Spell-check is a bitch. As soon as that wavy red line appears, I have the unhinged desire to correct the error rather than admit defeat to the computer. I know how *rhythm* is spelled! *Rhythme*. Crap. *Rythm*. Nope . . . *Rhythm*. Okay, got it. Now, on with the rest of the sentence . . .

What was I writing about?

If there isn't a name for that corrective desire, there should be. How about *inflamorecte*?[3] Or *deletequint*. Maybe *spellcheckitis*? Whatever the desire to correct oneself is called (so many possibilities), that same drive and persistence is absolutely embedded in this wine.

Luckily you don't have to spell-check the name of it. It's correct—Fumé Blanc—which is really Sauvignon Blanc aged in a slightly different way. It's like a homonym for Sauvignon Blanc, but you won't have to search for the meaning or check the spelling. Nothing but pure satisfaction from knowing that you have correctly read the label of this wine and that everything is right with the world. Your persistence has paid off and now you can indulge in a wine that speaks the same language.

There's so much to discover in the glass.

---

3 From the Latin root *recte* meaning "correct," of course. What did you think it meant?

We look for shooting stars, hike to mountain peaks, and converge in places like Niagara Falls.

CLOUDSLEY CELLARS
TWENTY MILE BENCH CHARDONNAY

WINERY PRICE: 🍷 🍷 🍷 🍷
BODY: MEDIUM
SWEETNESS: DRY
ATTITUDE: ETHEREAL

Pair with: Poached Atlantic salmon, clam chowder, watching rainbows or the aurora borealis

---

What is it about watching the northern lights, a.k.a. the aurora borealis? It is a natural wonder that we get to see only in the cold night sky, and when it happens, these lights are magnificent to behold. A friend of mine makes jewellery out of photos of the northern lights, showcasing their rare beauty. For those of us who have never seen these lights in person, rainbows offer a similar sense of wonder.

These natural phenomena have captivated humanity for as long as there have been humans. If there is anything that we share with our ancestors, it is awe in the natural world. We look for shooting stars, hike to mountain peaks, and converge in places like Niagara Falls.

This wine has a similarly ethereal quality. The flavours are delicate and dance around weightlessly with each sublime sip.

Of course, perspective is a factor. If this wine is too cold, the aromas won't dance as freely. There will also be less of them. As with the northern lights, the proper conditions create magic. Let the wine warm slightly, and it will put on a beautiful show.

It can be a steep
learning curve, so
don't rush.

KEW VINEYARDS MARSANNE VIOGNIER

WINERY PRICE: ♟ ♟
BODY: MEDIUM
SWEETNESS: DRY
ATTITUDE: STUDIOUS

Pair with: Charcuterie, pasta with carbonara sauce, reading a complex mystery novel

---

WHITE

This wine is a total smarty-pants. There's a lot going on with it, but if you ask for details, it may not talk. It also likes secrets. The harder you try to get information out of it, the more it will resist. It doesn't matter how much you sniff or aerate, this wine reveals its mysteries slowly. Though this may be infuriating at first, it will keep the tenacious sipster extraordinarily busy. This wine rewards deep study.

If you haven't studied a wine before, this wine provides the perfect opportunity. The more time you spend with it, the more you'll understand it. It can be a steep learning curve, so don't rush. Trust that at some point things will just click. When it does, enjoy the rush of excitement that comes from learning something new.

Sipster's Tip: If this wine is too cold, it will *really* hide itself. This wine really benefits from a little warming in the glass. Also, try it in a glass that you would normally use for red wine. This will help bring out the complex aromas.

If only we
could open
our noses
more.

KONZELMANN OLD VINES RIESLING

WINERY PRICE: 🍸 🍸 🍸
BODY: LIGHT
SWEETNESS: DRY
ATTITUDE: SAUNTER

Pair with: Sweet-and-sour pork chops, beet salad, garden parties

This is the R. Murray Schafer of wine.

Imagine a slow walk through a beautiful garden. Everything is there, from the garden hoses to the highest leaves on the trees. Walking through a well-tended garden or an organized botanical garden is often thought of as a visual feast. *Wow! Look at those blossoms. The flowers are so beautiful. Those leaves look fantastic in that light.* The visual elements seem to overtake the other senses, making us think that all gardens must look beautiful to be beautiful.

If only we could open our noses more. There is a whole olfactory world to explore, and this wine will remind you of that with every sip. This is what I learned from Canadian composer R. Murray Schafer, who encouraged people to focus more on how the world sounded than on how it looked. He often signed his books "The seats for the world concert are free! Listen to the symphony!" to encourage people to spend more time listening to the world around them. He designed epic works of musical theatre to explore this multi-sensory approach to experiencing music and performance art.

This Riesling will help you understand what that is all about. There is almost no way to ignore the beautiful clarity of colour in the glass, nor the lovely scents emanating from it. As you sip, the intense flavours are impossible to ignore, but there is also something else—the texture. Experience it as you sip and swallow.

This wine will sharpen all of your senses, making your world look and feel a little different if you take the time to enjoy it.

The instruments sound like ones you've heard before (pianos, guitars, drums, etc.), but there's something different about them.

LIGHTHALL CHARDONNAY

WINERY PRICE: 🍷 🍷 🍷
BODY: LIGHT
SWEETNESS: DRY
ATTITUDE: AMIABLE

Pair with: Oka cheese, charcuterie, the Rheostatics album Music Inspired by the Group of Seven

This wine is like a friend with a weird sense of humour. Some people will get their jokes, which may confuse other people, especially if they don't understand the context. I experienced something akin to this when I first heard Rheostatics, particularly their *Group of Seven* album. If you have no context for it, it seems kind of . . . weird. The instruments sound like ones you've heard before (pianos, guitars, drums, etc.), but there's something different about them.

This wine is a little funky at first, but trust me—it will win you over. Many wine lovers, educated to seek out "100-point" wines (whatever those are), have an idealized concept of what a wine's typicity should be; they will be confounded by these aromas and flavours. But sipsters aren't afraid of novel experiences, and you shouldn't be either. This is what makes wine interesting and, sometimes, challenging. Your concept of what makes a beautiful wine may change, though it won't happen instantly. You'll need a few sips—perhaps another glass—to really get into it.

Like a friend with an odd sense of humour, you will come to love what makes this wine unique. There's no reason to cling to outdated value systems. Try something outside of your comfort zone. You won't regret it.

Guessing what someone's intentions are isn't always fun, and for some people, it's downright stressful.

MAGNOTTA CHARDONNAY

WINERY PRICE: 🍷 🍷 🍷
BODY: MEDIUM
SWEETNESS: DRY
ATTITUDE: DIRECT

Pair with: Pasta with cream sauce, crab cakes, romantic dinners

It is nice to know how people feel about you. This removes some of the mystery and, yes, some of the drama. Guessing what someone's intentions are isn't always fun, and for some people, it's downright stressful. Not everyone can be socially outgoing in the moment. This one is for the introverted, shy sipsters.

This wine will tell you how it feels about you without holding anything back. If it's totally smitten with you and wants to take you out to a romantic dinner, there will be no guessing about intentions. Your first kiss is coming sooner than you think.

The confidence of that directness is evident in every sip. This is an oaked Chardonnay, and it makes no apologies for being exactly what it is. It makes no apologies for its sensuality either, with lots of texture and nuance to keep you interested during the second course.

Take your time and enjoy the moment together.

All the social
cues you've used
to indicate that
you're leaving the
conversation now
are for naught.

PELLER ESTATES
SIGNATURE SERIES RIESLING

WINERY PRICE: 🍷 🍷 🍷 🍷
BODY: LIGHT
SWEETNESS: OFF-DRY
ATTITUDE: SOCIABLE

Pair with: Pork schnitzel, jerk chicken, backyard parties

If you have a friend who enjoys wine, there is a strong probability that they've tried to persuade you to try a Riesling. At some point in their wine education, they were taught about the benefits of a Riesling-based wine diet, and now, they need to spread the love of Riesling around like a holy relic. All the social cues you've used to indicate that you're leaving the conversation now are for naught. Even as you step backward to the door, they *still keep talking to you*, making you feel the smallest spark of guilt for not sticking around to see what they need to tell you about Riesling *this* time.

Fortunately, this wine speaks for itself. You don't have to be a four-star general in the sipster brigade to get the appeal of this one. Its smooth, appley texture is approachable, and it has no austerity or rough edges. It might even make conversations with your Riesling friend a little more concise: you're already in agreement.

And when you bring a bottle to your next party, *you* might be the one who can't stop talking about it.

Dry. Super dry. Like walking for hours through the desert kind of dry.

PENINSULA RIDGE BEAL VINEYARD RIESLING

WINERY PRICE: 🍷 🍷 🍷
BODY: LIGHT
SWEETNESS: DRY
ATTITUDE: WITTY

Pair with: Pork chops with apples, poutine, puns

Me: Hey, look, they have watermelon juice at the supermarket now.

Son: Hmmm . . . so it's . . . *water* then?

Me: Well, no . . . it's juice . . . you know, from a watermelon.

Son: . . .

Me: Yes, fine, okay, it's water.

My son's sense of humour closely resembles this wine. Dry. Super dry. Like walking for hours through the desert kind of dry. Like listening to a three-hour lecture on semiotics kind of dry.

But it's also hysterically funny. While it seems obvious that the juice of a watermelon is, in fact, water, it isn't always so obvious. Great comedians use this kind of lateral thinking all the time. They take something obvious or mundane and make you think about it in a way that's both fresh and recognizable. You think that they'll go in one direction and then BAM, you get hit with something you weren't expecting. That's what makes it entertaining.

When you see the word *Riesling* on this wine's label, you may think, *Rieslings are sweet. That's what makes them good.* So you buy it and take it home and open it and then—

BAM.

Like it's wearing a
tuxedo jacket with
board shorts and
colourful high-tops.

REIF ESTATE WINERY KERNER RESERVE

WINERY PRICE: 🍷 🍷 🍷
BODY: MEDIUM
SWEETNESS: OFF-DRY
ATTITUDE: JOVIAL

Pair with: Salty cheeses, spicy chicken wings, getting messy

There is a time and place for formal things. It's often assumed that wines are supposed to occupy the more formal settings when you're celebrating something (the same goes for that expensive suit or cocktail dress in the back of your closet). Wine is for the priceless moments. For everything else, there's beer and a pair of blue jeans.

This wine is not formal. Though it looks very serious with its tall, slim bottle and Germanic label, there's nothing stodgy about the way it tastes. It is a bottle of ribald fun held back by a wee cork. It tastes like it's wearing a tuxedo jacket with board shorts and colourful high-tops. The flavours are wonderful to behold, but the texture is what really makes it pop; it's beautifully rounded without any rough edges.

Place a bowl of assorted spicy chicken wings in the middle of the table and let the party begin.

These moments feel amazing enough that you want to shout them out to the world.

RENNIE ESTATE WINERY
CHRISTINE CHARDONNAY

WINERY PRICE: 🍷 🍷 🍷 🍷 🍷
BODY: FULL
SWEETNESS: DRY
ATTITUDE: F$%K YEAH

Pair with: Veal, fresh lobster, arriving

When you have well and truly arrived, you'll know it. Have you just closed an amazing deal? Gotten a raise or promotion? Landed a new contract? Maybe you just graduated with your PhD? Just got married?[4] Whatever it may be, you've got something to really celebrate. Life can throw a lot at you, and these moments feel amazing enough that you want to shout them out to the world.

This wine is the oenological declaration that you have arrived. It's your fist pumped in the air when you realize what just happened. It's the camera flash as you get out of that beautiful car and onto the red carpet. This wine is your moment.

But you don't have to wait until these things happen. Sometimes just being exposed to that level of positivity can help propel you to greater heights than you even thought possible. If success has been slow to arrive and you feel like you aren't even close to your goals, pause for a moment and smell the aromas coming out of your glass. Just the smell of this wine may be enough to stir you up again.

---

4 Or divorced? Hey, it happens. Doesn't mean you can't celebrate, though . . . right?

This wine will
sharpen your
senses like a
chisel.

SANDBANKS PINOT GRIGIO

WINERY PRICE: 🍷 🍷
BODY: LIGHT
SWEETNESS: DRY
ATTITUDE: BRISK

Pair with: Shrimp rings, green salads, hot topics

What do you call the opposite of doomscrolling? This wine. It will stop you in your tracks and make you look at the world around you. Although no wine (or anything else) can make you stop scrolling for long if that's your thing.

This wine will sharpen your senses like a chisel, making it the perfect before-dinner bevvy or accompaniment to appetizers or salad courses. Were your taste buds a bit tired? A sip of this wine will slap them awake real quick. They will stand at attention—ready for duty, SIR!—willing to perform whatever tasting tasks they are assigned.

You are now primed to take time and really appreciate the flavours you're about to enjoy. This is what a brisk wine can do when you line it up correctly at the start of a meal. Sipsters who love to have their palates challenged with beautiful flavours will want to set this wine at the centre of their tables.

Or maybe that amazing walk down the Beltline Trail to the old brickworks.

STONEBRIDGE CHARDONNAY

WINERY PRICE: ♟ ♟ ♟ ♟ ♟
BODY: FULL
SWEETNESS: DRY
ATTITUDE: CAREFREE

Pair with: Sautéed scallops, grilled chicken, Chopin nocturnes

This wine is a carefree bicycle ride through the park in early September. You will taste the sunshine. You will feel the warm breeze, tinged now with the impending chill of October. You will anticipate the presence of great friends and remember the good times you've had together.

The hue of this wine will pull you in, transporting you to that time you drove through wine country or biked along the parkway near the Niagara River when all the colours were changing. Or maybe that amazing walk down the Beltline Trail to the old brickworks. This wine is like VR for your taste buds.

The aromas will take you away too, in a beautifully lilting way that will make you think you're having an out-of-body experience. Only the magic of aromas can make your brain do this. Let those memories come back, think about them briefly, and then let them float away, carefree into the ether as you take your first sip. There is no need to dwell on them. Allow the aromas to call in new thoughts to replace them.

With complexity like this, you'll have lots of time to think.

Didn't win that lottery like you were hoping? No problem.

SUGARBUSH VINEYARDS RIESLING

WINERY PRICE: 🍷 🍷 🍷
BODY: MEDIUM
SWEETNESS: DRY
ATTITUDE: GRANDIOSE

Pair with: Pork stir-fry, schnitzel, parading

When the day has been long and hard and the discussions difficult, this is the wine to declare yourself victorious over another day. Didn't win that lottery like you were hoping? No problem. You still have your freedom! March around your living room and be proud of your accomplishment.

Even small victories are worth celebrating. You have everything to gain from acknowledging the little things that contribute to life's worth. Doing so is a great way to stay positive, and this wine will get you into the positive vibe. The aromas jump out at you as if to say, "Hi! Hope you're having a great day!" The flavours are so approachable you can almost hear them asking, "What is the most *amazing* thing you did today?" It's a difficult outlook to ignore even when you're not necessarily in the mood.

You are living your best life and showing gratitude and all that yadda yadda, but fuck all that—take a sip of this and celebrate your version of victory.

Now is now and then was then, which makes it all just a tad awkward, doesn't it?

TAWSE SKETCHES CHARDONNAY

WINERY PRICE: ♀ ♀ ♀
BODY: MEDIUM
SWEETNESS: DRY
ATTITUDE: WISTFUL

Pair with: Chicken cordon bleu, sautéed veggies, looking through high school yearbooks

The uniquely insightful philosophical wisdom of each week's episode of *The Simpsons* often offered small golden nuggets of truth. One episode depicted a sign on the kids' school's yearbook office that read "Immortalizing your awkward phase."

Truer words were never put to cartoon poster board. Paging through one's own yearbook conjures a unique feeling that can be fun for some, traumatizing for others. You know who the people pictured are (or were) and you're well aware that you were one of them. Except that now you don't feel exactly the same as you did then. If then was now, you'd be all over those memories and know exactly what you should have done. Except that now is not then, now is now and then was then, which makes it all just a tad awkward, doesn't it?

Tasting this wine isn't awkward at all, but there is a hint of wistful nostalgia in its aromas and flavours. It is a lovingly oaked style of Chardonnay, one that some of us may remember from years past, as if trying to relive the glory days when the average restaurant didn't know squat about wine and even the casual sipster could get a reasonably good bottle for a lot less money.

However, that was then. And right now, you've got an amazing wine in your glass.

The biggest trope in this genre of reality television is *the reveal* at the end.

VINELAND ESTATES WINERY ELEVATION RIESLING ST. URBAN VINEYARD

WINERY PRICE: 🍷 🍷
BODY: MEDIUM
SWEETNESS: OFF-DRY
ATTITUDE: REVELATORY

WHITE

Pair with: Chips and dip, BBQ chicken, home renovation shows

A partner of mine used to love watching those home renovation shows. The biggest trope in this genre of reality television is *the reveal* at the end. This part guaranteed some drama. Would they love it? Would they hate it? Would they fight over it? Can you feel the tension?

Suffice it to say that, for a while, everything in our house became a play on the reveal. When dinner was ready, it wasn't just placed on the table but rather was unveiled in an overly dramatic fashion. It was amazing how something that worked on TV became silly in real life. What it never became was boring, and we certainly got some laughs out of otherwise mundane daily tasks.

This wine will bring an element of surprise to your life when you sip it. The beautifully bright texture will liven anything up with its acidity. Take the first bite of your meal and enjoy. Then have a sip. *And now*, you will see your newly renovated food, with even MORE flavours than you had before! *Wow*! Can you believe it? That's *amazing*!

Unlike the home reno shows, this wine will actually enhance your eating experience for real with every sip, without painting over beautifully varnished hardwood or taping wallpaper into place just to make it look good on TV.

Some people have the same lunch every day or prefer to put their coats on the same hanger in their closet.

WAYNE GRETZKY ESTATES
WHISKY OAK AGED CHARDONNAY

WINERY PRICE: 🍷 🍷
BODY: MEDIUM
SWEETNESS: DRY
ATTITUDE: COMFORTABLE

Pair with: Cedar-planked salmon, corn chowder, patio conversations

Familiarity breeds comfort. There's a certain ease when we experience something frequently. You might place your keys in the same place, perhaps a bowl by the door, when you return home from work. Some people have the same lunch every day or prefer to put their coats on the same hanger in their closet. While some people crave the adventure of trying something new, many take comfort in this predictability. They like what they like, and they take comfort in knowing it will always be that way.

This Chardonnay has everything you need in a truly comfortable wine. It is pleasantly balanced with the familiar flavours of a wine that has spent some time in an oak barrel. It has that round, smooth texture that tells you to sit back and chill—everything is fine. The flavours aren't going to push you around or demand a food pairing. You can enjoy this wine without anything but a good book or a great conversation.

Still, there's no need to worry about this wine getting boring. If you let this one sit in your cellar for a few years, its evolution will certainly keep your boredom at bay when you finally pour yourself a glass.

ROSÉ WINES

The word about rosés is finally getting out there. No longer do we assume that these pink-hued wines are merely sweet and superficial. Sipsters know that they can be as serious and complex as wines from any other category.

Modern rosés are *not* the melted pink Popsicle juices of the past. This was a style for a long time, but it's no longer as common as it used to be. You can still buy stragglers of this ilk at the LCBO, mostly from other wine regions in the world, but they are not common among legit Ontario VQA wines.

Versatility is the name of the game for modern rosés, which can pair with casual or formal settings and a ton of different foods. Rosé can even stand in as the main wine with foods that are otherwise difficult to pair. With rosé, the question is not "What foods go with this rosé?" but rather "What foods *don't* go with this rosé?" That might be a more difficult question to answer.

It's the red romper with yellow polka dots in a sea of little black dresses.

KONZELMANN PEACH WINE

WINERY PRICE: 🍷 🍷
BODY: MEDIUM
SWEETNESS: MEDIUM
ATTITUDE: REBELLIOUS

Pair with: Pastries, beef hoisin stir-fry, blind tastings

This wine is the rebel. It's the red romper with yellow polka dots in a sea of little black dresses. It's the blue shirt in a sea of white. It's the only bottle in the cellar that thinks differently. When you're stuck in a vinous rut, don't know what to serve, and are a bit worn out by all of the regular choices, this is the rebellious newbie that will reinvigorate your palate, amuse your friends, and provide a great experience at the same time.

Wine made from fruit can elicit ire among more traditional wine lovers. "It can't be called *wine* because it's not made from grapes. It's etymologically incorrect . . ." Blah blah blah. Bunk. If it can do the same thing as a wine—taste amazing, pair well with food, and provide a beautiful tasting experience—then that's wine enough for me. Sipsters love a unique tasting experience that challenges them with something different, and this wine absolutely delivers. Plus, there's the added bonus that your traditional wine friends will never have tried it before, so you'll be offering something totally new.

If you want to be a bit of a rebel yourself, bring this wine to a blind tasting. Everyone will be able to peg it as a peach wine, but nobody will be able to argue against how good it is.

My gut tells me
I'm wasting a lot
of time keeping
my phone within
reach.

OXLEY ESTATE WINERY PINOT ROSÉ

WINERY PRICE: 🍷 🍷 🍷
BODY: LIGHT
SWEETNESS: DRY
ATTITUDE: EFFICIENT

Pair with: Cheese and baguettes, picnic sandwiches, digital detoxes

I believe the amount of energy we spend trying to keep our phones nearby is far greater than the amount of energy we would exert locating our phones upon hearing a notification. For every four trips to another room to find your phone, there is maybe one notification that needs your response. There is no way to test this theory, of course, but my gut tells me I'm wasting a lot of time keeping my phone within reach, grasping for it to make sure that it's there, going back to the kitchen to get it after sitting down in the living room.

Not that having it close by provides much benefit. My text message alert is the sound of a light sabre ignition that I bought years ago and never updated. Unless it is set to silent, I don't miss many texts. Except for the one time I missed three messages while watching an episode of *The Mandalorian*. Not everything is fail-safe, and our relationship with technology is often far from efficient.

This wine, on the other hand, wastes no time. You won't be baited into following aromas or flavours that aren't really there. It's light, herbal, and fruity, with a finish that will last until your next sip. This is the real deal. You might even forget about your phone for a glass or two.

ROSÉ

The first sip is that dunk in the lake you've been thinking about for months.

PENINSULA RIDGE BEAL VINEYARD CABERNET ROSÉ

WINERY PRICE: 🍷 🍷
BODY: MEDIUM
SWEETNESS: OFF-DRY
ATTITUDE: SUMMER

Pair with: Genoa salami, quiche, rope swings into the lake

This is your ticket to summer. If this wine doesn't do it for you on your patio, balcony, or back deck, nothing will. Sell your house. Move to a new place, somewhere you can properly experience this wonderful season.

When you get there, you'll be greeted by the amazing aromas, flavours, and refreshing textures of this wine. The first sip is that dunk in the lake you've been thinking about for months. It's your first time taking the boat out for a rip, accelerating out of your driveway on your first motorcycle ride through the warm summer air. It's a slow walk through a farmers' market. It's all of these things, new and familiar as the changing seasons.

Great wines have the ability to transport us to different times and places through their aromas and flavours. They plug into our memories somehow, even if we've never tasted them before. The aromas of this wine certainly have that power, and what a treat that is!

RED WINES

I am of the opinion that Ontario red wines are underappreciated. If you've bought a book on Ontario wine (like the one you're reading now), you probably already agree with me. It is my hope that the wines in the following pages will fire you up to help spread the word about Ontario reds among your friends, family, and—if you are so inclined and it comes to it—the random people you pass on the street.

The preconception that Ontario cannot ripen red grape varieties as well as other regions is frankly nonsensical, given that Ontario is producing Pinot Noirs on the highest level and at a price that rivals those produced elsewhere. Ontario Gamays are equally fantastic, and there are a growing number of Ontariones[5]—a unique and fantastic style made from grapes that have been dried, which is sure to catch the attention of wine lovers throughout Canada.

The joy of red wine in Ontario right now is that it no longer has to imitate classic red wine regions elsewhere and can focus on becoming the best red wines *Ontario* has to offer.

5 This is an Amarone-style wine from Ontario—thus, Ontarione.

You may feel the need to step closer and get a better look at the tiny details.

13TH STREET WINERY
SANDSTONE GAMAY

WINERY PRICE: 🍷 🍷 🍷
BODY: MEDIUM
SWEETNESS: DRY
ATTITUDE: ARTISTIC

Pair with: Rotisserie chicken, grilled pork tenderloin, discussing art

A great work of art is fun to appreciate; it can draw you in, almost forcing you to look again, dig deeper, and pay closer attention. You may feel the need to step closer and get a better look at the tiny details in a compelling painting or sculpture. You may have to listen a little more attentively to the musician. You may have to taste the food more slowly to take in all of the flavours. It's not that anyone tells you to do these things. You just know. Simple or complex as a work may seem, if it's well constructed, it takes more than one glance to take in everything it has to offer.

This Gamay will draw you in the way only great art can. Without knowing why, you may feel pulled to take extra time admiring it in the glass. Take that time. You may need extra sniffs to enjoy all of the aromas. Engage your sniffer just a little longer. You may need to take an extra sip to appreciate the flavours. Savour the wine's finish as it slowly slips away.

None of these impulses should be unique to this wine. What is unique, however, what makes it a great work of art, is its texture. The tannins are soft and silky in your mouth, giving your palate a comfortable place to rest and allowing you to reflect on the flavours and aromas you just experienced. Take your time. It's worth it.

RED

This is where I am going to get a lot of stuff done. It is ready for me, and I'm ready for it.

BACHELDER SAUNDERS
"WARREN SAUNDERS 100" PINOT NOIR

WINERY PRICE: 🍷 🍷 🍷 🍷 🍷
BODY: MEDIUM
SWEETNESS: DRY
ATTITUDE: PROGRESSIVE

Pair with: Duck confit, pasta with mushroom sauce, getting ready

Home offices used to be less common. In the "before times," fewer people worked from home on a casual or part-time basis. If they had a home office, it was probably for a side hustle or a semi-professional hobby, like writing. Teachers and professors surely had studies for reading or grading assignments, but the average person had little need for a designated workspace at home.

During and after the pandemic, home offices became a lot more common. Perhaps you set one up as well? I know people who converted their spare bedrooms into offices while others used their dining room tables as their workplace Grand Central. I am sure some people stuffed home workspaces into random corners, under stairs, in basements, attics, or garages. I saw more than a few friends proudly post photos of their new office spaces on social media. Some of them were very creative, and they all seemed like "before" photos, as if this was the start of something very interesting. This is where I am going to get a lot of stuff done. It is ready for me, and I'm ready for it. Let's *do* this! Go!

This wine feels like it has that same potential. It's that feeling between the time when you are finished your preparations and the time that you actually start to work in that new space. You are excited to get started. You've popped the cork. Enjoy what comes next after all of your hard work.

RED

The humidity level might be higher *outside* the hot tub, but still.

CALM THE
FRANC DOWN!
VQA NIAGARA PENINSULA VQA

BELLA TERRA CALM THE FRANC DOWN!

WINERY PRICE: 🍷 🍷 🍷
BODY: MEDIUM
SWEETNESS: DRY
ATTITUDE: JOYOUS

Pair with: T-bone steak with Montreal steak spice, roast pork with blueberry compote, hot tubs

---

If there isn't already a name for the feeling one gets when they first slip into the soothing, swirling waters of a hot tub or hot spring, there should be. That feeling is amazing.

Even in the height of summer, when it's hot and humid, that feeling still exists for whoever decides to climb into the tub at the end of a hard day. The humidity level might be higher *outside* the hot tub, but still, the desire for that feeling (whatever we're going to start calling it) remains. It can be healing to immerse yourself like that, but *healing* doesn't capture the full scope of the sensation.

This wine does (I'm still open to suggestions on what to call it). This wine embodies the feeling of being enveloped by something special and gives you the same sense of safety, comfort, and familiarity, even if you haven't tasted it before. You will get that feeling, whatever it's called (just shout it out when you think of it), from the first sip to the very last drop. Reaching that final drop may take a while; just like a soak in the hot tub, there is no need to rush. You can take your time with and savour all the beautiful moments between your first and last sips.

RED

I have a friend who lives far, far away and there are days or weeks when I don't hear from her at all.

2021
PINOT NOIR
VQA PRINCE EDWARD COUNTY VQA
ESTATE GROWN AND BOTTLED
UNFILTERED

Casa·Dea

CASA-DEA PINOT NOIR RESERVE

WINERY PRICE: ♟ ♟ ♟
BODY: MEDIUM
SWEETNESS: DRY
ATTITUDE: HIPPIE

Pair with: Penne with pesto, pan-fried cremini mushrooms, be-ins

When you just need to turn off, relax your weary mind, and float downstream, this is the wine to have in your glass. And not because of the alcohol content. We aren't talking about intoxication; we're talking about silencing your phone notifications, hitting Do Not Disturb or turning the device off completely.[6] I have a friend who lives far, far away and there are days or weeks when I don't hear from her at all. She does not respond. She does not acknowledge. She does not reach out.

This may freak some people out, or at least make them a little perturbed, but I understand. My friend needs that time to herself to disconnect. She knows that she doesn't have to respond just because her phone vibrates. I admire that about her and try to emulate it. Sometimes I succeed. Reading helps.

Being enamoured with a wine helps too, but not just any wine will do the trick. The wine has to have an inner dimensionality to it. Drinking it should feel like staring at a billion stars in a space the size of your hand. There is peace in the universe, and you are witnessing it.

This wine is that inner peace.

RED

6 Gasp. Do phones even *do* that?

It's one of those
hugs where your
perspective subtly
changes as you
pull away.

THE FOREIGN AFFAIR DREAM

WINERY PRICE: ♈ ♈ ♈
BODY: MEDIUM
SWEETNESS: DRY
ATTITUDE: COMFORTABLE

Pair with: Homemade pasta sauce, cheese boards, your favourite jeans

---

Comfort means different things to different people. What some people find comfortable would make others question their sanity. It's a matter of perspective and personal preference. Maybe comfort can come from a particular place, such as a room in a house. Certain styles of music may be more comfortable than others. Perhaps certain foods elicit that comfort feeling. You know comfort when you see it.

Or smell it, which is exactly what happened when I first poured this wine. I didn't even have to put my nose into the glass. I knew that this was going to be the wine equivalent of a hug. One of those long embraces where the world slows down for a second and all that matters is the brief connection you are sharing with another person. It's one of those hugs where your perspective subtly changes as you pull away.

If you were having a bad day before the hug, your day has brightened, if only a little.

It has more to do
with attitude than
with power, real
or implied.

HENRY OF PELHAM
SPECK FAMILY RESERVE PINOT NOIR

WINERY PRICE: 🍷 🍷 🍷 🍷
BODY: MEDIUM
SWEETNESS: DRY
ATTITUDE: REGAL

Pair with: Mushroom risotto, soft cheeses, saluting

What does it mean to be regal? Perhaps in Canada, we think of regality as having to do with being in government or maybe watching people waving in a parade. Being regal, or having that kind of comportment, does not always have to be so formal.

There are instances where being regal is more stylistic than factual. It has more to do with attitude than with power, real or implied. When Loreena McKennitt crosses the concert stage to the Celtic harp waiting for her in the centre, she walks as though she's the queen of the theatre. Then she plays the most beautiful music, accompanied by her band of merry troubadours. She commands the songs with a smile, and it is done. If that isn't regal, then I've misunderstood the word.

This wine expresses the same regal quality. The aromas march from the glass with an authority that is simply part of its nature. It will not bow to anyone, but you, loyal sipster that you are, will bow as you put your nose into the glass, unknowingly acknowledging the wine's royal nature. It will command you to take a sip, and you will obey.

By the end of this bottle, you might very well be swearing allegiance to it.

RED

It isn't really that
complicated. Nor
should it be.

KEW VINEYARDS GAMAY

WINERY PRICE: ♈ ♈ ♈
BODY: MEDIUM
SWEETNESS: DRY
ATTITUDE: PLEASING

Pair with: Chicken burgers, grilled sausages, date nights in

How to enjoy this wine:
1. Open the bottle.
2. Pour a glass.
3. Look at the wine.
4. Smell it.
5. Take a sip.
6. Allow the beautiful aromas and flavours to waft gently over your soul, surrounding you with a deep appreciation of all the things life has to offer, and bask in the gratitude that you are able to partake.
7. Repeat Steps 4 through 6 as needed, with food, until the bottle is empty.

It isn't really that complicated. Nor should it be. Still, I'm convinced that some people skip a few of these steps, Steps 3 and 4 in particular. At the beginning of the evening, they pour and sip. As the evening goes on and the wine starts to warm hearts and blunt minds, sipping sometimes evolves into gulping or, worse, chugging.

Not all wines are so amenable to being accessed, but this wine isn't hidden in any way. You don't have to wait for it in the cellar. There is no peak "drink now" phase for which you must hold off lest you incur the wrath of the wine snob. Yes, this wine will change and evolve over time (most wines do), but it will be there, ready and willing, whenever you need it. Make sure to spend as much time as you need on Step 6, for as long as it's in your glass.

RED

I know what you're thinking. *There's no way*. But there is.

KIN VINEYARDS
CARP RIDGE PINOT NOIR

WINERY PRICE: 🍷 🍷 🍷 🍷
BODY: LIGHT
SWEETNESS: DRY
ATTITUDE: OTHERWORLDLY

Pair with: Mushroom arancini, roast duck, adventuring

Friend: "Oh, this is fantastic—I love it!"

Me: "Glad you like it."

Friend: "I would totally buy this again."

Me: ". . . You didn't buy it."

Friend: "But it's really good! So glad I got this one."

Me: "It was a sample sent to me—"

Friend: "It's beautifully balanced . . ."

Me: "—by the winery."

Friend: "Totally on my shopping list again. Where's it from? We have to go there on my next trip to Niagara."

Me: "Funny you mentioned that . . ."

Sometimes, we can be so overwhelmed with information that it muddles our memories and recollection of circumstances. This is a beautiful Pinot Noir that may well overwhelm you with its beauty. The aromas are gorgeous, the texture is silky, and there is complexity at every stage of the tasting experience. It's the real deal when it comes to Ontario Pinot Noir.

And yet there's something slightly different about it. This wine is from the Ottawa region. I know what you're thinking. *There's no way*. But there is. This wine will show you.

RED

Forks may drop. Wine may slosh to a stop mid-swirl.

REDSTONE WINERY MERLOT

WINERY PRICE: ♟ ♟ ♟ ♟
BODY: MEDIUM
SWEETNESS: DRY
ATTITUDE: PROVOCATIVE

Pair with: Lamb skewers, chocolate tarts, making a point

Here's how to start an argument at your next wine tasting. Say something like, "I had this great Merlot from Ontario the other day."

Forks may drop. Wine may slosh to a stop mid-swirl. Corks may mysteriously become airborne near your head as tasting books are slammed and wine apps are closed with extra terseness. This is a provocative statement.

And yet, it shouldn't be. All Merlot needs to be happy is a little clay in the dirt. Redstone must have found that clay under their vineyard because their Merlot seems quite at home. This is the key to finding the best wines. Where a wine is grown determines how good it has the potential to become.

Serve this wine at your next tasting, and you just may finally get an apology from whoever threw that cork at you.

RED

It's a shockingly
affordable introduction to
a style of winemaking
I call Ontarione.

THE MAGICIAN

HE KNOWS HOW TO USE
ALL THE TOOLS AT HIS DISPOSAL
TO COME UP WITH CLEVER PLANS
NO ONE ELSE WOULD THINK OF
INTRODUCING OUR
~ KILN DRIED~

2019 Shiraz · Pinot Noir

VQA · NIAGARA PENINSULA · VQA

REIF ESTATE WINERY
THE MAGICIAN SHIRAZ/PINOT NOIR

WINERY PRICE: 🍷 🍷 🍷 🍷
BODY: FULL
SWEETNESS: DRY
ATTITUDE: HUMBLE

Pair with: Roast lamb, dark chocolate, sharing with friends

This wine doesn't know how good it is. How does it appear so humble?

There could be many reasons. Perhaps it doesn't receive much attention through Reif's marketing or social media? Perhaps, when you walk into their lovely wine shop, you don't notice it immediately on the shelf? Perhaps, perhaps, perhaps . . .

The price must help. It's a shockingly affordable introduction to a style of winemaking I call Ontarione,[7] in which the grapes are dried before being fermented like a normal red wine. The result is a very rich style that makes you want to check how much you paid, just to be sure.

But the appeal doesn't end there. This wine is highly approachable and will satisfy a wide spectrum of wine enthusiasts, perhaps even those who say that they don't like red wine. There are no jagged edges to this, and it can be sipped without food, as white wine lovers often prefer.

This wine will leave you wondering how it escaped your notice for so long.

RED

---

7 A mash-up of *Ontario* and *Amarone*, from Italy, where this *appassimento* technique was made famous. This one is only partially Ontarione since a percentage of the grapes were dried for the vintage that I experienced.

What if you tell
and suddenly
everyone wants it?

ROSEWOOD SHOULDERS OF GIANTS CABERNET FRANC

WINERY PRICE: 🍷 🍷 🍷 🍷 🍷
BODY: MEDIUM
SWEETNESS: DRY
ATTITUDE: ENERGETIC

Pair with: New York strip loin, grilled peppers, campfires

Some wines are so good that you don't want to tell anyone about them. What if you tell and suddenly everyone wants it? The wine will sell out more quickly each year until it becomes so expensive and hard to find that only collectors will be able to get their hands on a bottle. If demand *really* soars, it might even reach that pinnacle of craziness where it becomes a "club only" wine and you have to join the winery's cult just to get your hands on it.

Oh, the *horror*!

Although Cabernet Franc doesn't have the cachet that other grape varieties may have in other parts of the world, in both of Canada's major wine regions, it is a sleeping giant. And Ontario is ahead of the game; Cabernet Franc is not only more widely accepted, but also achieving greatness in the bottle. (Of course, as a sipster, you already know how good it is.)

At some point, a winery will hit it out of the park at a major wine competition or get a vintage listed at a prestigious restaurant in a top market. Then wine lovers and critics everywhere will finally recognize Cabernet Franc on a whole new level.

This wine could be the one.

RED

The surface may seem simple, but the structure below is complex.

STONEBRIDGE CABERNET SAUVIGNON

WINERY PRICE: 🍷 🍷 🍷 🍷 🍷
BODY: FULL
SWEETNESS: DRY
ATTITUDE: HEAVY

Pair with: Lamb stew, bison burgers, Lateralus *by Tool*

Like all things subjected to the whims of fashion, music changes over time. It changes for a lot of reasons, but technology is certainly one of them. The music that has lasted longest may sound thin to modern ears, but if a song is well written and constructed, it should have that staying power. That's why the Beatles, Dolly Parton, and the Foo Fighters are still popular today.

Tool appears to be on the same timeless track. For whatever reason, the band's fans span a broad demographic that includes metalheads and string quartet players alike. There is so much information loaded into their albums that every listening experience is slightly different; each time you listen, you pick up on new sounds, phrases, and motifs that you may have missed before. The surface may seem simple, but the structure below is complex.

On the surface, this wine is a lovely Cabernet Sauvignon that's accessible and easy to understand. Give it a few extra minutes swirling in your glass, hours in the decanter, or years in the cellar, and you will be rewarded with more depth and complexity that will make it difficult for you to understand why you didn't buy more of it when you had the chance.

Sipster's Tip: This is a great contender for your cellar if you are looking for something to put away for 5–10 years.

RED

They might enjoy skydiving but only ever drink one brand of beer.

STONEHOUSE VINEYARD MARQUETTE

WINERY PRICE: ▼ ▼ ▼
BODY: MEDIUM
SWEETNESS: DRY
ATTITUDE: ADVENTUROUS

Pair with: Tomato-based casseroles, savoury salads, group selfies

Some people love adventure. They crave it. They look for new paths to hike, new roads to drive, new hills to climb. And it's not limited to physical activities. Trying new foods or flavours can be an adventure. As can reading a different type of book. If this is your first book about wine, you are on an adventure right now!

Other people get solace from experiencing the same things—the same lunch every day, the same view out the window, and the same shows on the TV. The comfort is in the predictability and there is absolutely nothing wrong with that, especially if it results in consistently positive mental benefits. I have always found it interesting that most people I meet enjoy being adventurous in some areas of their life while keeping some things the same. They might enjoy skydiving but only ever drink one brand of beer. They might go out of their way to go on different hikes each week but always be in bed by exactly 9:00 PM.

However adventurous you feel, if you enjoy trying different wines, this one will be thrilling for you. It is made with a grape variety called Marquette (uh, what?) and is grown in Lochiel (um, where?) and will take you on a true taste adventure. If you haven't googled Lochiel by now, it is in Glengarry County in eastern Ontario, exactly nowhere near the big wine-growing regions in Niagara or even Prince Edward County. (Yes, there are lots of Ontario wineries that are not in Niagara.)

Sip this wine and post a selfie to show everyone your adventure.

RED

You are a better
person because of
the way you interact
with them.

TAWSE CABERNET FRANC

WINERY PRICE: 🍷 🍷 🍷
BODY: LIGHT
SWEETNESS: DRY
ATTITUDE: POSITIVE

Pair with: Steaks that sizzle, Greek salad, romantic movies that sizzle

---

Some people just make you feel like you're a pleasure to be around. It is almost like they enhance you in some way. You are a better person because of the way you interact with them. They listen to you. They don't take things the wrong way. They ask questions and are interested in what you're doing. It's a mutually beneficial relationship that, given the chance to unfold over years or decades, makes you both better people than if you hadn't known each other.

Essentially, that's what all great wine and food pairings should be. Wine should make the food taste better and the food should make the wine taste better. It isn't that they weren't good individually, but that they both achieve greater things when they are together.

This wine is for your casual steak dinner. The dinner on its own would be delicious. New York strip loin, sizzling on the barbecue, maybe with some mushrooms and onions, and perhaps a little steak sauce of choice. What will put it over the top is sipping this Cabernet Franc. There will be no awkward silences in the conversation and both will rise to the occasion.

RED

You both enjoyed
the same amazing
sunshine today.

TAWSE PINOT NOIR

WINERY PRICE: 🍷 🍷 🍷
BODY: LIGHT
SWEETNESS: DRY
ATTITUDE: MINDFUL

Pair with: Braised chicken, pork kebabs, relaxing at the end of a full week

Some wines are there to remind you about what you're missing in life. They transcend time and space to tell you how amazing it is in Tuscany or southern France. These wines taste fantastic, even as they taunt you for not living in their grapes' old haunts. Too bad for you.

This Pinot Noir would never taunt. It will remind you that this moment *right here* and *right now* is everything. You worked hard this week. You got shit done. You had an amazing first date with a wonderful new person. You found time to read a great book and binge watch a few episodes of your favourite show. You had a *great* week.

This is what a special local wine can do. You and the wine both come from the same place. For all you know, the grape-vines responsible for this wine had a pretty great week too. Perhaps this was the week in late spring when new buds started to push out shoots. Perhaps this was the week at the end of the summer when the grapes turned colour. Maybe this was the week the fruit was harvested. You both enjoyed the same amazing sunshine today.

Enjoy your now time. Tomorrow is coming soon enough.

RED

If it has anything to
say, what it says is
only a starting point.

FIFTY MISSION CAB
2021 CABERNET SAUVIGNON

VQA NIAGARA PENINSULA VQA

THE TRAGICALLY HIP FIFTY MISSION CAB CABERNET SAUVIGNON

WINERY PRICE: 🍷 🍷 🍷 🍷
BODY: MEDIUM
SWEETNESS: DRY
ATTITUDE: CURIOUS

Pair with: Steak salad, grilled peppers, living life fully and completely

Everything about this wine, from the label to the bottom of your glass, is a deep dive.

If you consider wine an art form like poetry, dance, or photography, consider what it is that makes art so compelling. If it has anything to say, what it says is only a starting point. Art is the beginning of a journey. It whets your appetite to learn more, go deeper, understand better.

This wine compels you to dive in. The images on the label are the obvious place to start. Of course, the name of the wine is a play on the name of one of the Tragically Hip's better-known songs. But there are other, less obvious things about it. It is made with a famous grape—Cabernet Sauvignon—but why? Where was it grown? Does it taste like other Cabernet Sauvignons you've tried? It's an elegant, well-rounded wine, but it's far from predictable. Why is that? What or who made it taste this way? Every time you sip it, it will taste a little different. Is that normal? What makes this wine so complex and compelling?

Take the deep dive, one sip at a time. See where it leads you.

RED

Of all the gazillion things that you can download, the feeling of soft velvet or rough burlap will not be one of them.

VINEDRESSERS CABERNET SAUVIGNON PETIT VERDOT

WINERY PRICE: ♥ ♥ ♥ ♥
BODY: FULL
SWEETNESS: DRY
ATTITUDE: LUSTFUL

Pair with: Prime rib, lamb stew, candlelit dinners

We don't really talk about textures as much in our daily lives. When we see images online, we might enjoy the saturated colours or unique perspectives, but they don't offer anything tactile. When we listen to music, the sounds don't translate into a textural experience (unless we happen to be standing near a subwoofer). Perhaps textures are more difficult to discuss because they can't be digitized. Of all the gazillion things that you can download, the feeling of soft velvet or rough burlap will not be one of them.

Even sipsters may not think about texture as much as they should. Wine appreciation focuses so much on aromas and flavours that other senses often get left behind. Even a wine's visual appearance isn't really given much airtime when it comes to critical evaluations, although many winemakers are quite proud of a vintage's colour.

Most often misunderstood, however, is a wine's texture. Why does it feel the way it does in your mouth? Is it grippy? Smooth? Rough or harsh? Is it rounded? Even though this wine is made with some of the biggest and most notoriously tannic grapes available, it won't feel rough as you might expect.

This wine has texture for days. It is sumptuous and satisfying to feel. Pair it with a great meal that includes a fine cloth dinner napkin and a lovely tablecloth and revel in the tactile pleasure of your evening.

RED

It's just that it isn't always the time and place for their chicanery.

VINELAND ESTATES WINERY CABERNET FRANC

WINERY PRICE: 🍷 🍷
BODY: MEDIUM
SWEETNESS: DRY
ATTITUDE: AMENABLE

Pair with: Artisanal pepperoni, pizza and wings, you know, like, whatever . . .

Some people have personalities you can only take in small doses. Every group has that friend who's great to have around for a party but may be a little overbearing during a quiet bistro dinner or backyard chat by the fire. It's not that you don't enjoy their company; it's just that it isn't always the time and place for their chicanery.

When you're fatigued by the bombastic tannins of big reds or the excessive acidity of popular whites and you just want a smooth, flavourful wine to relax with, this is your bottle. Got food? Snack away. Not hungry? That's great too. Sip away. The value of this wine is its amenability to any situation. It isn't going to argue. It will go along with whatever occasion you have in mind without making a fuss.

This wine can totally handle your carefree wandering. A wine this versatile and easygoing is rare in any wine region, so when you find it, always buy multiples.

RED

There are no
harsh tannins
to disrupt your
flow or get in
the way of your
enjoyment.

WAYNE GRETZKY ESTATES BACO NOIR

WINERY PRICE: ♈ ♈
BODY: MEDIUM
SWEETNESS: OFF-DRY
ATTITUDE: AMICABLE

Pair with: Burgers, sausages, white wine drinkers

For me, the big appeal of subscriber streaming services like Netflix is that there are no commercials to sit through. I've always found the ads to be an intrusion. They break up the flow of a story, disrupt the pace, and kill the excitement. I want to find out how the killer is going to get caught, not hear the long list of possible side effects for a hair loss medication I don't need. No, thank you.

For some people, the tannins in red wine are annoying commercials that bring their enjoyment to a halt. People who find red wines too harsh or bitter are often put off by the tannins, the natural fruit-sourced elements that can contribute to a red wine's texture. Although Baco Noir has never been on the A-list of grape varieties in the wine world, in the right place and handled the right way, it can be lovely. So lovely, in fact, that people who don't like red wine (or *say* that they don't like red wine) will probably find this one quite approachable. There are no harsh tannins to disrupt your flow or get in the way of your enjoyment.

It's like being able to enjoy the things you watch on TV, without advertisements.

You look up to discover that the restaurant you're in is closing and you are the last customers inside.

WESTCOTT VINEYARDS ESTATE PINOT NOIR

WINERY PRICE: 🍷 🍷 🍷 🍷
BODY: MEDIUM
SWEETNESS: DRY
ATTITUDE: LOVESTRUCK

Pair with: Lamb sirloins, roasted veggies, second dates

Sometimes you meet someone and suddenly, you can't for the life of you remember how to breathe. This person has an energy about them, or a look to them, that tells you how special they are; you *need* to get to know them more. The world around you narrows into focus. You tune out the chatter in the room to home in on what that person is saying. Your sense of the world has diminished to such an extent that after talking for what seems like a half-hour, you look up to discover that the restaurant you're in is closing and you are the last customers inside.

If we make assumptions about the beginnings of romantic relationships based on what we see in movies, we might think that all men become idiots and all women become withdrawn. Everyone handles these situations a little differently, but our reactions are probably a lot more universal than we like to believe.

This bodes well for this wine, which will have you caught in a lovestruck daze for as long as you have some in your glass. You won't be able to pull your senses from it. Suddenly, the other wines on the table won't be so interesting anymore. I had the pleasure of being introduced to this wine on two separate occasions thousands of miles apart, and the effect was the same each time.

Hello. It's very nice to meet you.

DESSERT WINES

When I worked on bottling lines, watching freshly filled and labelled vintages travel past me on the conveyors, the potential future of each bottle used to amaze me. Instead of seeing just a bunch of wine, I saw each bottle as a special occasion. Each one was going to be part of somebody's great dinner with their family, a special date night, or a gift to a treasured friend. Each one was going to be purchased and appreciated by whoever chose it. I used to imagine all the ways these wines were going to be enjoyed.

One day, we were bottling a dessert wine. Other than the obvious gift-giving or after-dinner scenarios, I struggled to find a similar set of occasions in this sweet wine's potential future. It seemed like a specialty food with severely limited uses. *There must be more to dessert wines than just being a sweet treat*, I thought. Some of them aren't even as sweet as you might expect!

Dessert wines can certainly be used to indulge your sweet tooth, but they also invite greater opportunities for creativity. Because we tend to drink them less often, we can be more inventive with our food and occasion pairings. Ontario is a legit, world-class wine region for dessert wines and, with that level of quality, there are abundant pairing possibilities. Try creating a dinner to pair with a late harvest wine . . . There are ways to do this and create an amazing experience. Sipsters love a good pairing challenge and dessert wines are a great way to get yourself thinking outside of the box.

Let's come up with something that will become so ubiquitous that everyone knows what to do with Icewine.

PILLITTERI KERNER ICEWINE

WINERY PRICE: 🍷 🍷 🍷 🍷
BODY: FULL
SWEETNESS: LUSCIOUS
ATTITUDE: TRADITIONAL

Pair with: Baklava, blue cheese and nuts, making memories

Why haven't Canadians established any traditions that involve Icewine? Canadian winemakers, especially those here in Ontario, are the best in the world at producing this unique style of wine. Notice that I didn't hedge this by saying that they are *among* the best in the world. Nobody else is doing this kind of wine on the same level; the terroir that makes up our wine-growing regions simply produces the best Icewines.

Perhaps sipsters should offer some suggestions to get things started. Any Canadian travelling with a reusable Tim's mug attached to their backpack with a carabiner should be able to speak about an Icewine tradition with the people they meet travelling abroad—"Ah, you're from Canada? I would love to enjoy a beautiful Icewine with [insert Icewine-drinking tradition or occasion here]!" Let's come up with something that will become so ubiquitous that everyone knows what to do with Icewine.

If there's an Icewine to inspire such a tradition, this is it. The fine folks at Pillitteri have a long history of making beautiful AF Icewines. Now let's make some new traditions to go along with them!

DESSERT

Whatever it was,
there was an olfactory
patina that came with
this authentic rusticity.

SOUTHBROOK THE ANNIVERSARY

WINERY PRICE: 🍷 🍷 🍷
BODY: MEDIUM
SWEETNESS: OFF-DRY
ATTITUDE: REVERENT

Pair with: Candied pecans, aged cheddar, an easy chair by the fire

When I was young, my parents bought everything at antique stores. It seemed like there were a lot of them in the small town where I grew up. Everything in these stores appeared ancient to me, and now that I'm older, I know I was right—those things were ancient, even then. My parents may not have had a lot of money, but there also weren't a lot of options when you needed bedroom furniture or a new dining set. These old things had a particular scent to them. Perhaps it was the varnish or the aged hardwood. Maybe the material had picked up scents from wherever the piece had been over the many years. Whatever it was, there was an olfactory patina that came with this authentic rusticity.

Later, when I was older, my parents bought a brand new dining room table and chair set. I hated it at first. It smelled weird. It smelled like new varnish or a lacquer of some kind. Blech. To my nose, it smelled chemical. When I was older, flat-pack furniture came with its own uniqueness without any reference (or reverence) to the past.

This wine manages to get it right somehow. It subtly hearkens back to a time when things were less disposable and built to last. It is a solid wine that does not require any assembly. It smells amazing and authentic. It is a wonder to behold and not just as a museum piece for the more nostalgic of us. It is a stunner of a wine that is destined to become a classic of its own.

Their songs make you pause—*What did he just sing?*—and then spend the next month thinking about them.

SUE-ANN STAFF ESTATE WINERY
VIDAL ICEWINE

WINERY PRICE: 🍷 🍷 🍷
BODY: FULL
SWEETNESS: LUSCIOUS
ATTITUDE: MYTHOLOGICAL

Pair with: Crème brûlée, apple pie, deep thoughts that only come in the first quiet moments after your guests have all left the party

This wine is like a deeply pensive lyric from the Tragically Hip. It will reveal itself, one star at a time.

Hip songs are deceptive and, like all great masterpieces, they appeal to many people on many different levels. On the one hand, you're rocking out on biker bar energy, with the dirty guitar sounds and straight-ahead grooves. On the other hand, you find yourself looking up references to legendary hockey games, who David Milgaard was, and what is so special about 100° longitude anyway? Their songs make you pause—*What did he just sing?*—and then spend the next month thinking about them. You may even learn something new about a town you visited once, an issue you didn't know about, or a chunk of Canadian history you weren't taught in school.

Like a great work of art, this wine can affect you on many different levels. On the one hand, you're imbibing a somewhat absurd amount of sugar, which is immediately pleasing and will appeal to many people. On the other hand, you find yourself searching for words and references associated with it: Who is the Ice Queen and what's so special about minus nine degrees Celsius? This wine will make you pause—*What did I just taste?*—and then spend the next few hours thinking about it as you gently crash from the sugar rush.

The Tragically Hip built their music on the terroir of Canadian culture. Icewine is made in the unique environment that is the terroir of the Ontario wine-growing regions. It's difficult to experience either one without wanting to delve deeper.

DESSERT

OUR RELATIONSHIP WITH ALCOHOL

Following the first set of pandemic lockdowns, many people began re-examining their relationship with wine and with alcohol in general. As Edward Slingerland notes frequently in his fantastic, and appropriately named, book *Drunk*, drinking alone can be dangerous. Unless your partner is a bartender, there's probably nobody serving you drinks or, more importantly, monitoring how much you're drinking when you're working from home. As we all know, "self-monitoring" means something entirely different from being aware of how many glasses of wine you've had in an evening. Slingerland suggests that societal pressures and obligations often act as a kind of safeguard against the overconsumption of alcohol. In cultures where wine is treated like a food and enjoyed only with meals, alcohol abuse in general is reduced. When those societal pressures are removed due to isolation at home, what are our safeguards?

Societal pressures (or encouragement) to drink more can come from social media, which can be a lifeline for human inter-action and information (although the accuracy of that infor-mation is certainly debatable). In the past, organized religion had a hand in guiding morals, but social media has taken on that role today. Slingerland notes that "our age is moralistic to a degree not seen since Queen Victoria's day" (page 289). It is difficult to discuss topics constructively with the binary "I'm right and you're wrong" of social media platforms. Shades of meaning go out the browser window and arguments become all or nothing. The nuances of an argument for or against anything are lost and difficult to ascertain. Just like in Victorian times, you are either a good person or branded as a witch. There is no in between. Similarly, at one time you were allowed to consume alcohol, or you weren't. This "moralism" resulted in the total prohibition of alcohol in Ontario and the rest of North America just over a century ago.

Being aware of our consumption habits, personally and as a society, should never be belittled or ignored. I have close friends who have given up drinking altogether, and I will always support them in this. The trend toward no- or low-alcohol wines illustrates a positive corrective measure to laissez-faire attitudes toward wine, depicted in many memes and bedazzled wine-shop T-shirts over the past decade. Dry January, once a fringe movement where people tried not to drink alcohol for the first month of the year, is a great way for anyone to judge their own habits and make choices for themselves.

I believe that a healthy philosophy for sipsters is to enjoy wine more for what it is than for what it does. The act of enjoyment is the appeal. Drinking too much seriously impacts our ability to enjoy wine, which is ultimately just a food and, for some, an important part of life. Pairing wine with food is the best way for sipsters to take the time to appreciate the nuances of wine, the skill it takes to make it, and the places it comes from.

When my son turned 19, I offered to make him a nice wine-paired dinner. It was a way of introducing him to good wine but also to set an example for how to handle alcohol. During discussions about drinking, I mentioned that for me, thinking about alcohol was important. I told him that I "drink to clink," meaning that when I have wine, it is with friends on occasions that we want to celebrate, clinking our glasses together to say cheers. I am well aware of the occupational dangers of writing about and marketing wine. I have seen others go down this road and take wrong turns, and I know it wouldn't be very difficult for me to do the same.

For sipsters, wine is a journey that's all about the senses, the mind, and the time spent with friends. Remember that with every glass.

ONTARIO WINE FROM AN OUTSIDE PERSPECTIVE

Sometimes, having an outsider's perspective on something can be reassuring and validating. We Canadians tend to more readily believe an opinion about something if it comes from outside of our own region. I grew up in Quebec, lived in the Maritimes for four years, and then moved to BC. I have visited every province in Canada and lived[8] in five of them. I first tasted a wine from Ontario in 1998, first toured Niagara in 2005, and have spent a lot of time in Ontario since. My parents and sister now live in an Ontario wine region and I've been studying Ontario wines intently for the past three years. With that, I can conclusively offer the following "outsider's" educated perspective on the wines from Ontario: You may not know how lucky you are. Ontario wines are fantastic.

There are so many reasons this is the case. I am well aware that since you have already purchased a book about Ontario wine, I may be preaching to the converted. However, what you are about to read might serve as a game plan for helping convince other, perhaps more skeptical, wine lovers of this fact.

ONTARIO WINES HAVE CHARACTER

In studying Ontario wine over the past three years, I have been amazed to see how cohesive the industry is. There is a remarkable amount of agreement among wineries about grape

---

8 Some of these were short term. I consider it a province I've lived in if I had a local phone number and received mail there.

varieties and styles. Chardonnay and Sauvignon Blanc can be deep and expressive while Pinot Noir and Gamay can be earthy and amazingly full. Cabernet Franc is also clearly at home in Niagara because some of the best wines I've ever experienced with this grape come from Ontario.

Some wineries are also using a newer technique called *appassimento* to make bigger and fuller wines. The technique of using dried, or partially dried, grapes was pioneered in Italy and used to make wine called Amarone. I remember hearing about trials using this technique on my first tour of Niagara in 2005 from Angelo Pavan at Cave Spring Cellars, but I never got to try a wine made that way until recently. Graham Rennie at Rennie Estate Winery and others have worked hard to develop technologies and techniques to dry grapes to make profoundly deep and expressive wines using Syrah, Merlot, and Cabernet Sauvignon to name a few. There are some beautiful wines made this way. I like to call this style Ontarione, and I'm certain that this style will become a widespread calling card for Ontario's wine industry on the world stage in the near future.

ONTARIO WINES ARE A GREAT VALUE

While it seems like everything is getting more expensive these days, Ontario wines are shockingly on par with their value.

"No, that's not true," says the skeptical wine friend. "We love Sauvignon Blanc and the ones from Ontario are always $20 or more. I can get one from Chile for $12. That's not good value."

To do this properly means comparing apples to apples, quality for quality. That $12 Sauvignon Blanc from the LCBO is owned by a multinational corporation that might also own smelters, a few shipping companies, some television stations, and other media companies in various parts of the world. That doesn't mean that the wine isn't good, but being made in such huge quantities means that it will be more homogeneous and taste less unique than one that was made from grapes grown on a smaller 80-acre vineyard and produced by a small team of people. There is also the economic argument that when you spend a few bucks more on a wine that is made locally, you are supporting the people who work locally and spend their money locally as well. They also pay rent and mortgages here, as well as contribute to the life of the community. That's where the real value is.

What makes it truly on par is that, when measured against similar quality levels from other wine regions, they are expressive in a way that is unique to Ontario. They are not trying to make a Sauvignon Blanc taste like Sancerre. They are making it like Ontario, and it costs less than a Sancerre.

ONTARIO'S WINE INDUSTRY KNOWS WHAT IT'S DOING

Brock University and the Niagara College Teaching Winery have trained some of the best people in the industry in Ontario through their programs, which focus on cool-climate oenology and viticulture. This alone makes Ontario a singular world-class wine region in Canada. The people who work in the wineries making and marketing wine have studied how to do it and are also teaching the world how things happen in Ontario. That translates into great experiences visiting wineries as well as amazing wines. When institutions support an industry, that industry is there for the long haul. So is the wine.

ONTARIO WINERIES ARE ACCESSIBLE

Visiting wineries in Niagara and other wine regions is a lot easier than it is in other Canadian wine regions. They are few and far between in Quebec and you'll spend a lot of time driving between them. There are just a few in Nova Scotia. There are plenty in BC, but only one highway connects most of them in the Okanagan, which is far away from centres like Vancouver and Calgary, Alberta, and makes day trips impossible.

No so for most of Ontario's wine industry. Niagara-on-the-Lake is an easy day trip from downtown Toronto. Travelling between wineries is quick and easy with the QEW on most days. You could easily spend multiple days just going to wineries that are off King Street between Grimsby and Jordan. The various towns have amenities for travellers and if they don't, St. Catharines and Niagara Falls have plenty of options for whatever you need. Throw in some stunning vistas of downtown Toronto when the skies are clear and you have a beautiful wine country experience.

So if you haven't been to Ontario's wine regions yet, what are you waiting for?

PASSION PLAYS

When I first started riding a motorcycle, I was struck by how often people would come up and talk to me about it. I would be stopped for gas, sitting on the curb eating a snack, and someone would come over to talk about riding, my bike, or their bikes. The longest conversations were with other riders who knew people who had a bike like mine and rode it across Canada but had a problem with the starter, or some other part. Wasn't that a pain, given that the model used European parts? It took forever to get them! And what kind of helmet was I using?

To be honest, I used to find these conversations a little annoying. It seemed like useless small talk most of the time. *Oh, you had a Triumph Daytona in the 1960s? You must really like oil leaks.* Some of the conversations were over quickly. *I have to get back on the road now—gotta go!* Other chats were really interesting, and I wish we could have spoken longer. I soon found that I came away from these conversations with new information: a little motorcycling history, a suggestion for gear, or the latest conditions on the road I was about to ride. I realized that this was really what storytelling was all about.

Storytelling is a fundamental part of being human. For thousands of years, we have learned about the world—how to be safe, how to survive, how to thrive—from stories told from one person to the next. When we are growing up, we hear stories to teach us about being safe outside, relating to other people. We hear stories from family members about their experiences and those of their ancestors and extended family members who lived before we were born. These stories help us learn about the world and where we come from, and influence our behaviours. We go to movies to experience fantastical, emotional, or humorous stories that entertain us. As we get older, the reason for stories may change, but I think the need to hear them continues. Anyone who craves a day with a novel may be looking to fill that need. Today, we stream movies, listen to podcasts,[9] subscribe to YouTube channels, or watch shows online to see and hear stories.

Stories are a big reason people share their wine experiences: "I had this fantastic wine the other night . . ." "You *have* to visit this winery! You won't believe the wines. . ." After taking years of wine courses, I can honestly say that learning about wine is so much easier when it is guided by genuine enthusiasm rather than by sales pitches, marketing tactics, or chasing scores. Storytelling is how we transmit these experiences.

Composer Philip Glass talked about using a new approach to an art, which he and the artists in his scene in the '60s and '70s were observing at the time. He remarked that "[a] new language requires a new technique. If you don't need a new technique, then what you're saying probably isn't new."[10] I want to introduce you to two sipsters who have developed new techniques for sharing their experiences. They have created tangible and meaningful expressions of their enthusiasm for wine and are offering them to wine lovers, contributing to the wine culture in Ontario, and Canada, in amazingly constructive ways. Here are their stories.

9 Such as *The Sipster's Wine Podcast*, available now on your favourite streaming platform. Ahem.
10 From *Glass: A Portrait of Philip in Twelve Parts* (2005), directed by Scott Hicks, 12:00.

LAURA MILNES
CRUSHABLE WINE CLUB

Laura is the ultimate Canadian wine maven. Where others choose to shout their views from the top of Mount Social Media, Laura opts to whisper it to small groups of people in a dedicated wine experience studio. She still uses social media effectively, but she has created other channels of influence where she can more tangibly contribute to Canadian wine culture without having to scream into the cyber-void hoping to be heard. Even though sipsters sometimes predict the future as a function of their passion for wine (as in "This wine will be great to try in 10 years"), I always hear Quentin Tarantino's line in *Four Rooms* when his character says, "The less a man makes declarative statements, the less apt he is to look foolish in retrospect." Keeping that in mind, I can conservatively declare that Canadian wine culture *will not be the same in the future* without Laura's contributions. The timeline will skew because of her.

Laura's interest in wine started around 2010, and she began to host regular tasting groups with friends in Calgary. They would each bring a bottle and then discuss them all in detail. They did blind tastings and even tried blind beer tastings. "That really opened my eyes to all the cool things you could do to assess taste and quality, and how so much of what we're led to believe is 'the best' is largely based on marketing." Eventually the discussions got more complicated, and Laura learned just how much there was to know about wine. "I hated that feeling of not knowing—it motivated me to learn, read, and study more."

She began to document her thoughts and discoveries about wine and food on her first blog, *Malolactic Interpretations*. "I was never all that consistent with it, which is why it was never that popular," she concedes. Still, wine was the spark that ignited her passion for writing. "The more I wrote, though, the more my writing improved—writing has always been a passion of mine, as it's always come naturally to me."

Laura's next move was a new website called Silk & Coupe, which launched in 2017. She had moved to the Okanagan Valley by then and started working in the wine industry. This provided contacts for her to dig further into wine culture, now from the producers' perspectives. She featured wines, wineries, winemakers, and people in the industry on her site, which also included a vlog on YouTube. Gradually, her blog posts and social media stories started to broaden to more diverse and controversial topics, some that most wine writers would not care to take on. "I feel like I have strong opinions that I need to share—even if they are polarizing." These topics included sexism in wine marketing, critiques of wine culture, and even the unhealthy aspects of social media—the very platform on which she was building her career.

To bring the debate into the real world, Laura organized an event called the Sensory Symposium, which was held at Okanagan College in Penticton in April 2019. It was the ultimate intimate tasting group experience, which brought a diverse selection of winemakers together to debate topics in panel discussions with an audience of enthusiasts and industry professionals. It was dialectical, constructive, and positively thought-provoking. Unlike traditional wine festival–style tastings, it was refreshingly honest and direct with frank conversations and interactions between panellists and attendees. The tastings and discussions were meant to challenge attitudes and philosophies about wine production and culture. Wine was a focal point but not the focus. Not everyone agreed on some issues, and that was okay. The intention was positive discussion, not about winning an argument or definitively solving the problem.

Laura is strong in her opinions and has no fear in sharing them. She has figured out the system of online marketing, staying clear of common "vinfluencer" tropes. Standing in a vineyard sniffing a glass to the side while posing in a beautiful dress is not in her vocabulary. Her socials are filled with a deliberate diversity of original memes, rants, and provocative photos.[11] There are also scenes of her and friends having actual, legitimate fun. There is no time to get the perfect pose or any need to use harsh filters. She uses sexuality in her online marketing not to draw attention to herself, but to authenticate herself, as if to say, *I'm not pretending to be someone I'm not—this is who I am*. She is careful to note that it is *her own* sexuality that she is using. She knows it works. "I've been cancelled, slandered, defamed. I've been called every name in the book." Wine culture tends to adopt a more formal and conservative appearance. Traditional wine images are loaded with upscale, formal occasions (dinners, receptions, country clubs) so jeans and a T-shirt don't fit. Talking about wine on Instagram while wearing an Orange Crush T-shirt or a string bikini challenges the norm for how a wine personality should appear. It will create reactions and generate views and comments. "It's actually wild the lengths people will go to, all in the name of shutting down opinions *they* don't agree with." Knowing how social media works, these strong reactions serve to increase her reach, on which she occasionally capitalizes with fun wine accessories. She has created small batches of products to sell such as T-shirts. One of these, the now-infamous Titty Tee, features Champagne coupes appropriately positioned on the front. She has created a wine club, called the Crushable Wine Club, which focuses on small Canadian wine producers. She also hosts private tastings called the Canadian Wine Tasting Experience.

Unfortunately for her detractors, Laura has an intellect, marketing savvy, and stamina that often outguns them. She responds to every single comment quickly and fairly. Her followers are loyal and often as outspoken as she is, which can quickly front-load the comments in her favour. This makes it abundantly clear that her detractors are in the minority.

The most common theme across Laura's work is challenging gatekeeping and snobbery in the industry. "I hear it

11 This means different things to different people. Showing Cava served in a sour glass is provocative to some while ranting about wine culture wearing Wicked Weasels might be more so to others. To each their own.

a lot from consumers who are incredibly intimidated by wine culture—it's even worse among peers." In an article about the use of sexuality in wine marketing, she questions the intentions of both sides of the debate while resisting the preachy tones that often accompany online opinion pieces.

"Never has it been more confusing to be a female working in wine marketing—the industry seems to be rife with gatekeepers (yes, still) dictating what's permitted and what's not, a dichotomy reminiscent to the tune of: if you're hot, you probably lack intellect. If you're smart, you shouldn't be sexual, or risk setting back women in wine decades."[12]

Laura's lack of fear to challenge the norms demonstrates her confidence in showcasing wines that *are good* rather than what *should be good*. This helps her maintain a completely open mind for wines that may otherwise be overlooked and sets her apart from most other wine personalities active today. If tasting a Canadian Pinot Noir and a similarly matched wine from Burgundy, she will decide her preferences for herself rather than be swayed by the accepted "wisdom" of Burgundy being the "superior" home of wines made from Pinot Noir. *Typicity* is not a word that holds much weight for her.

Bottom line—Laura knows who she is. She knows what's good and what isn't, and will call out bullshit at its first whiff. She has figured out how to communicate her ideas about the Canadian wine that's worth knowing about and purchasing. Canadian wine culture will never be the same.

---

12 Crushable, "Sex and Wine: Where Progressivism and Misogyny Collide," February 7, 2022, https://www.crushable.club/opinion /sex-and-wine-where-progressivism-and-misogyny-collide.

CARL AND MIRA BOUCHER
CARL'S WINE CLUB

If Canada were hiring a high priest of wine, Carl Boucher's resumé would put him at the top of the committee's list of candidates. The level of energy and enthusiasm with which Carl approaches wine is fascinating, if only because it could power a small city—if it were possible to harness. His passion borders on religious fervour, and he talks about wines like he is preaching a sermon. Instead of fire and brimstone, it is tannin and acidity.

Carl hails from Chicoutimi, Quebec, which is as far removed from any Canadian wine country as it is possible to be while still existing below the 50th parallel. In the late 1990s, he chose the Université Laval to study international geography and started working in a restaurant to help pay for his education. Fortunately, the restaurant had a large and diverse wine cellar. "The love for wine," says Carl, "started as the connection between the geography and where the wine comes from." This drew Carl to the cellar any chance he could get, spending his breaks looking at the bottles more closely. Since this was before easy online searches on a smartphone, Carl had to research these places in books. His favourite was *The World Atlas of Wine* by Hugh Johnson and Jancis Robinson, which became his bible.

Fortunately for Carl, one day the wine director of the restaurant went on vacation and never returned, leaving the cellar without a manager. The restaurant owner told him, "You spend all of your time in there anyway, why not start managing the wines?" Carl dropped his degree ambitions and took any and all wine courses he could find to augment his insatiable thirst for knowledge. The next five years were a whirlwind of restaurant and hotel positions in Montreal. In 2004, he was recruited by a Calgary-based restaurateur who was looking for a francophone to help open a French restaurant. Barely able to speak English at this point, Carl bravely left Quebec and made the move west.

He arrived to find a restaurant scene that was very different from the one he'd left. "Calgary was booming at that point," explains Carl. It was a stark contrast to the perpetually depressed economy of Quebec relative to the rest of Canada. As the French restaurant he was working on took shape, he had access to wines from other restaurants within the same company, which included some of the top wines of the world. "We had Romanée-Conti on the wine list," Carl recalls.

In February of 2013, Carl met Mira Motet, who was working as the associate director of development at the Schulich School of Engineering at the University of Calgary. Mira was born in Bucharest, Romania. Her family moved to Victoria, BC, in 1994, and she graduated from the University of Victoria in 2008. After graduating, she ran the alumni calling program at UVic before progressing to fundraising for other universities and private schools. She moved to Calgary soon after. A friend of Mira's published an online magazine that featured an article on a different bachelor and bachelorette each week. Mira and Carl were featured on the same week and the editor arranged for them to meet on a blind date, which clearly went well.

Always an entrepreneur, Mira invented a sensory table for children with the goal of selling them to schools and school boards. She made them in small batches in the garage in her spare time. Unfortunately a Canada Post strike coincided with the launch of her product online, which resulted in commitments to order when the strike was over. With no money coming in, prospects for that business sank before the strike was over. "I learned about e-commerce with that," recalls Mira. "I had an incredible coach that used to work with Microsoft that understood customer experience and how to get people to engage online." This experience would be extremely valuable in the near future.

By 2014, Carl was tired of the hospitality grind. Tired of missing out on special family days, he started a consulting company focusing on cellar management, purchase strategies, and cellar appraising, which allowed him to have a "regular" nine-to-five type of job for the first time. One of the other projects that Carl's company started was a wine club that focused on international wines. This came to the attention of Gregg Saretsky, the CEO of WestJet, who hired Carl in 2015 to revamp the wine program for the airline's on-board service. As Carl related, this was a big "WTF moment" because one of WestJet's caveats was that he needed to focus on Canadian wine, which Carl knew nothing about. Having been immersed in the international wine world for so many years, Canada had been off his radar thus far. It was an opportunity for him to learn and he dove into the task, quickly becoming amazed at how good some of the wines were.

By 2019, with a growing family and looking for new adventures, Mira suggested that she and Carl start something about wine online. For a career sommelier in hospitality, Carl had trouble imagining how wine could be presented in an effective way online. "What you do with wine is personal—it's emotion," Carl says. Still, in the back of his mind, he knew it could be done. He had watched Gary Vaynerchuk's *Wine Library TV* back in the day and was aware of other online marketing strategies in play through the teen years as e-commerce started to adapt with new social media technologies. The idea for Carl's Wine Club was born, and by early 2020, they were ready to launch. Carl hosted his first virtual tasting for a birthday party in February that year.

Of course, timing is everything. It can make or break a business, as Mira's experience with the children's sensory table only a few years prior had demonstrated. This time things were different. As the pandemic restrictions set in, Carl and Mira found that they were already set up and ready to go with everything they needed to offer online wine appreciation and sell club memberships. Mira's online marketing savvy and organization skills paired with Carl's engaging online personality and passion for wine at just the right time to launch the club, which quickly gained over 1,000 members in the first four weeks.

The heart of the club revolved around offering wines from a featured winery from either Ontario or British Columbia each week. They livestreamed virtual tastings at 8:00 PM eastern time on #WineWednesdays, which also sometimes included interviews with winemakers and wine personalities. They used social media to build a community of Canadian wine lovers from coast to coast until they could go live with the first offer of wines from Bottega Wine Studio, a small producer from BC's Similkameen Valley. They have featured a steady stream of wineries from Ontario and BC ever since.

The live, interactive element of their videos has made them both accessible personalities to their club members, who have a familiarity with both Carl and Mira. "We just feel like we know them," says Mira. "It's like that amongst the members too. They've been swapping tastings notes and giving advice about which wines to drink now. It's really a community. I think that's really special." Carl adds, "At the end of the day, Carl's Wine Club is all about members."

The choice to livestream rather than produce edited videos drives home that accessibility. When members comment directly, Carl and Mira can respond immediately. Livestreaming is also unedited and highly improvised, making them seem like real people rather than impersonal talking heads on a TV. Sometimes there are long pauses or technical issues, which humanize them even more. Since no additional editing time is needed, they have been able to produce streams regularly without adding hours of editing and post-production to their workloads.

Shortly after launching Carl's Wine Club as the pandemic set in, the couple made the decision to move their family to the Okanagan Valley in BC and be based directly out of wine country. Alongside the club, they saw an opportunity to help wineries with online marketing efforts that they knew were going to be critical for wineries to succeed during the pandemic.

They were determined that Carl's Wine Club be focused on Canadian wines and not just BC. Carl's experience with WestJet had brought him contacts at many Ontario wineries. He travelled frequently to Ontario for tastings and to gather media for their online presence. In meeting so many winery owners and winemakers across the country, Carl decided that they needed a vehicle to showcase the depth of Canadian wine in a marquee event of some kind. While each wine region had their own wine festivals, there was nothing that showcased all wine regions at the same time. Having sampled so many wines from across the country, Carl is one of the very few people with that diversity of Canadian wine-tasting experience.

The concept for the Pan-Canadian Wine Masterclass came about in July 2023. With the help and encouragement of Marcel Morgenstern at Bella Terra Vineyards in Niagara-on-the-Lake, the event was put together quickly with tickets going on sale in short order. The tasting was hosted by Carl at Bella Terra and featured a round table of winery owners and winemakers including Brian Schmidt from Vineland Estates Winery, Keith Tyers from Closson Chase, and Rob Hammersley from Black Market Wine Co. The ticketed event featured wine tastings from Ontario, Nova Scotia, and BC. Carl and Mira hope to make this an annual event that switches back and forth between Ontario and BC each year to build a broader wine industry community across the country and increase awareness about Canadian wine.

The Bouchers are passionate about Canadian wine and have found an outlet for that passion. Carl's Wine Club is actively generating a wine subculture that will influence a generation of Canadian wine lovers that has the potential to outlive the club itself. Where they go from here is a mystery but one that will surely evolve over time, just like the wines they love so much.

ACKNOWLEDGEMENTS

Thank you to my fellow sipster tasting crew—Adrienne, Avery, Megan, and Stephanie—without whom I would be drinking, uh, I mean *tasting*, wine on my own, which isn't nearly as much fun.

Thank you to the team at TouchWood Editions for continuing to make such cool new wine books.

Thank you to all of the amazing people in the Ontario wine industry, who have been extraordinarily generous with their time to do tastings, record podcast interviews, and send samples of their amazing wines. Cheers!

SIPSTER'S WINE NOTES

WINE NAME: _____

PRICE: _____ ♀ ♀ ♀ ♀ ♀

BODY: LIGHT / MEDIUM / FULL

SWEETNESS: DRY / OFF-DRY / MEDIUM / SWEET

ATTITUDE: _____

What I paired it with: _____
_____
_____

Where I was: _____
_____
_____

Who I was with: _____
_____
_____

What kind of experience it was: _____
_____
_____
_____
_____

SIPSTER'S WINE NOTES

WINE NAME: _____

PRICE: _____ ♆ ♆ ♆ ♆ ♆

BODY: LIGHT / MEDIUM / FULL

SWEETNESS: DRY / OFF-DRY / MEDIUM / SWEET

ATTITUDE: _____

What I paired it with: _____

_____

_____

Where I was: _____

_____

_____

Who I was with: _____

_____

_____

What kind of experience it was: _____

_____

_____

_____

_____

SIPSTER'S WINE NOTES

WINE NAME: _____

PRICE: _____ 🍷 🍷 🍷 🍷 🍷

BODY: LIGHT / MEDIUM / FULL

SWEETNESS: DRY / OFF-DRY / MEDIUM / SWEET

ATTITUDE: _____

What I paired it with: _____
_____
_____

Where I was: _____
_____
_____

Who I was with: _____
_____
_____

What kind of experience it was: _____
_____
_____
_____
_____

INDEX